THE OIL AND GAS INDUSTRY GUIDE

KEY INSIGHTS FOR INVESTMENT PROFESSIONALS

Jens Zimmermann, CFA

© 2016 CFA Institute. All rights reserved.

All rights reserved. No part of this publication may be reproduced or transmitted in any form or by any means, electronic or mechanical, including photocopy, recording, or any information storage and retrieval system, without permission of the copyright holder. Requests for permission to make copies of any part of the work should be mailed to: Copyright Permissions, CFA Institute, 915 East High Street, Charlottesville, Virginia 22902.

CFA®, Chartered Financial Analyst®, CIPM®, Claritas®, and GIPS® are just a few of the trademarks owned by CFA Institute. To view a list of CFA Institute trademarks and the Guide for the Use of CFA Institute Marks, please visit our website at www.cfainstitute.org.

This publication is designed to provide accurate and authoritative information in regard to the subject matter covered. It is provided with the understanding that the publisher is not engaged in rendering legal, accounting, or other professional service. If professional advice or other expert assistance is required, the services of a competent professional should be sought.

978-1-942713-33-3
March 2016

ABOUT THE AUTHOR

Jens Zimmermann, CFA, is an equity analyst on the buy side for VP Bank. His research has been featured in the print media and on news channels (CNBC and Bloomberg TV). Mr. Zimmermann started his career as a fundamental research analyst for Standard & Poor's before he moved into sell-side equity research for UniCredit Bank, where he covered small- and mid-cap companies from the industrial, material, utility, and transportation sectors. He continued his career as a buy-side equity analyst for ABN AMRO, where he analyzed European and North American oil and gas companies from all subsectors before moving to energy consulting firm Wood Mackenzie as an energy market analyst for the Middle East. Mr. Zimmermann holds a MBA degree from the University of Munich and an MA degree in global finance from the University of Denver.

CFA INSTITUTE INDUSTRY GUIDES

THESE OTHER INDUSTRY GUIDES ARE AVAILABLE FROM CFA INSTITUTE

THE ASSET MANAGEMENT INDUSTRY
Owen Concannon, CFA
April 2015

THE PHARMACEUTICAL INDUSTRY
Marietta Miemietz, CFA
November 2013

THE AUTOMOTIVE INDUSTRY
Adam Kindreich, CFA
August 2015

THE REIT INDUSTRY
Irfan Younus, CFA
April 2015

THE MACHINERY INDUSTRY
Anthony M. Fiore, CFA
September 2013

THE TOBACCO INDUSTRY
Ade Roberts, CFA
April 2014

INDUSTRY GUIDES ARE AVAILABLE AT WWW.CFAPUBS.ORG/LOI/IND

CONTENTS

Industry Structure and Energy Subsectors   1

Energy Demand Trends   5
    Energy Sector: Highly Cyclical and Correlated with Oil and
        Natural Gas Prices   5
    Global Energy and Oil Demand Trends   7

Oil Producers: E&P and IO Companies   11
    Oil and Gas Production   11
    Oil and Gas Reserves   12

Oil Services Providers   15
    Contract Drilling   16
    Oil Field Services   22
    Engineering and Construction   26

Refining and Marketing   30
    The Refining Process   30
    Simple Refinery   34
    Complex Refinery   36
    Refinery Configuration Drives Refining Profits   37
    Regional Product Balances   42
    Refining Margins   43

Industry Themes   45
    Shale Oil and Shale Gas   45
    Liquefied Natural Gas   51

Financial Analysis   56
    Oil and Gas Accounting under US GAAP and IFRS   56
    Financial Statement Analysis   72

Valuation of Energy Stocks   80
    Absolute Valuation   80
    Market-Based Valuation Multiples   87

Energy Sector Performance   98
    Outperformance since 2000   98
    Underperformance since 2009   99
    Relative Subsector Performances   101

Industry References **104**
    Books 104
    Periodicals 105
    Research and Data Providers 106
    Governmental and International Agencies 107
    Trade Associations and Industry Training 108

Appendix 1. Average Annual Reference Prices **110**

Appendix 2. Monthly Baker Hughes Rig Count **112**

Appendix 3. US Companies Using Successful Efforts vs. Full-Cost Accounting **115**

Appendix 4. Energy Subsector Constituents **116**

Appendix 5. Balance Sheet Structure of Energy Subsectors **118**

Appendix 6. Financial Indicators Related to the Income Statement **120**

Appendix 7. Historical Energy Subsector Valuation, One-Year Forward Valuation Multiples **123**

INDUSTRY STRUCTURE AND ENERGY SUBSECTORS

The energy sector is complex and consists of several subsectors that provide various services that are central to the process of getting hydrocarbons out of the ground and delivering them as various refined products (such as gasoline, diesel, and heating oil) to customers around the world. The oil and gas industry can broadly be broken down into four segments:

- Upstream—exploration and production for oil and natural gas

- Midstream—primarily pipeline companies involved in processing, transporting, and storing the produced oil and gas

- Downstream—refining and marketing operations, which refine crude oil into various products and market these refined products, such as gasoline or heating oil, to retail customers

- Oil field services—providers of such client services as exploration and production and business refinement

In addition to pure exploration and production (E&P) and refining and marketing (R&M) companies, which focus either entirely on upstream or downstream activities, are integrated oil companies, which combine both lines of business as they refine the produced crude oil from their own oil fields in their own refineries and market their refined products. Although most refiners also have marketing operations, some do not. For example, in the United States, the names of some integrated oil companies appear on the signs at many local gas stations, but the name may be only licensed; the integrated oil companies often do not wish to run retail stores and/or sell gasoline directly to consumers. **Exhibit 1** summarizes the value chain in the oil-producing and -refining segment.

Over the past century, oil producers (E&P and integrated oil companies) have increasingly outsourced different oil exploration and production activities to specialized drilling, oil field services, and engineering and construction companies. Doing so allows them to benefit from improved efficiency and from the specialized expertise that these focused service providers can offer to their client base.

In the oil and gas exploration and production business cycle, oil producers are the principals that subcontract services to oil services agents during the development of their oil and gas reservoirs. The principals (E&P and integrated oil companies) own and sell the produced hydrocarbons and own the yet-to-be produced reserves that

Exhibit 1.   Oil Production and Refining Value Chain

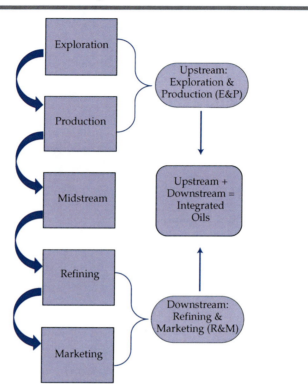

are still in the ground. A significant portion of the capital spending of oil producers (their expenditures for the exploration, development, and production of hydrocarbons) represents the revenue stream for the oil services industry.

Similarly, on the R&M side of the oil and gas value chain, the capital spending related to building, upgrading, or maintaining refining and petrochemical operations provides the revenue source for engineering and construction (E&C) companies.

The interdependent relationship between oil and gas producers and their service providers can best be explained through the life cycle of an oil and gas field, as shown in **Exhibit 2**. As the oil and gas field is monetized through the standard exploration, appraisal, development, and production phases, the drilling, oil field services, and E&C companies support the field operations and infrastructure development by offering the requisite services and products at each stage of an oil and gas field's life cycle via subcontracts. These companies offer a range of drilling, production stimulation, and E&C services for their clients in the up- and downstream industries.

Industry Structure and Energy Subsectors

Exhibit 2. Required Services during the Life Cycle of an Oil and Gas Field

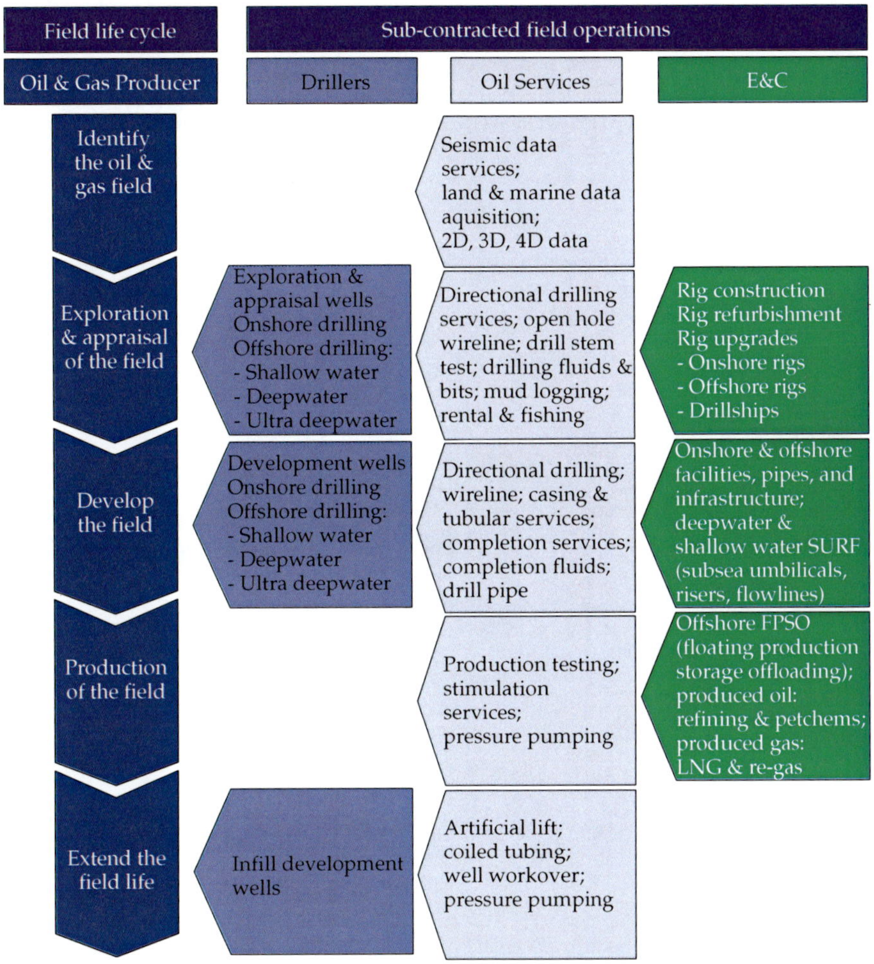

Field life cycle	Sub-contracted field operations		
Oil & Gas Producer	Drillers	Oil Services	E&C
Identify the oil & gas field		Seismic data services; land & marine data aquisition; 2D, 3D, 4D data	
Exploration & appraisal of the field	Exploration & appraisal wells Onshore drilling Offshore drilling: - Shallow water - Deepwater - Ultra deepwater	Directional drilling services; open hole wireline; drill stem test; drilling fluids & bits; mud logging; rental & fishing	Rig construction Rig refurbishment Rig upgrades - Onshore rigs - Offshore rigs - Drillships
Develop the field	Development wells Onshore drilling Offshore drilling: - Shallow water - Deepwater - Ultra deepwater	Directional drilling; wireline; casing & tubular services; completion services; completion fluids; drill pipe	Onshore & offshore facilities, pipes, and infrastructure; deepwater & shallow water SURF (subsea umbilicals, risers, flowlines)
Production of the field		Production testing; stimulation services; pressure pumping	Offshore FPSO (floating production storage offloading); produced oil: refining & petchems; produced gas: LNG & re-gas
Extend the field life	Infill development wells	Artificial lift; coiled tubing; well workover; pressure pumping	

Based on the industry categorization, this industry guide distinguishes and analyzes six subsectors within the energy sector:

1. E&P
2. R&M
3. Integrated oil (IO)

4. Oil field services (OS)

5. E&C

6. Contract drilling (CD)

The guide does not include any midstream companies in the analysis.

ENERGY DEMAND TRENDS

ENERGY SECTOR: HIGHLY CYCLICAL AND CORRELATED WITH OIL AND NATURAL GAS PRICES

Demand for energy depends primarily on economic activity, as broadly reflected by global GDP growth. When the global economy enters a recession, economic activity declines and the demand for energy falls accordingly. During times of economic expansion, more energy is needed to fuel growing manufacturing and industrial output in energy-intensive industries. Therefore, demand for oil and gas and derived refined products is highly cyclical, and energy consumption usually tracks an overall volatile economic cycle.

Oil prices are mostly driven by global energy demand trends. Global oil supply tends to be fairly inelastic, especially during periods when energy demand declines significantly, such as when the global economy enters a recession. When global economic activity contracts, oil demand reacts in a relatively short time with reduced economic activity as well. In order to defend oil prices, OPEC (Organization of the Petroleum Exporting Countries) has historically reduced output when global economic activity falls but only with a time lag and often with limited success, as seen during the 2008–09 global recession. Because energy demand trends strongly affect oil prices, oil is a highly cyclical commodity that tracks global economic growth (i.e., GDP) trends, as shown in **Exhibit 3**.

Increased fiscal spending requirements in the Middle East after the Arab Spring have elevated the dependence on oil export revenues in most OPEC countries, which has also limited their willingness to quickly cut production in order to defend oil prices. As a result, when OPEC does not defend oil prices but rather attempts to maintain its global market share in an oversupplied oil market, which happened in 2014 and in 2015, oil prices continue to fall. Prices then have to find a new floor based on a new supply and demand equilibrium at lower price levels. During the oversupplied oil market in 2014 and in 2015, West Texas Intermediate (WTI) oil prices collapsed by 76% from $107/barrel (bbl) in June 2014 to $26/bbl in January 2016. In this case, new oil supply from US onshore shale oil production was not matched by the OPEC production cuts required to keep the global oil market in balance.

Oil prices are a key driver of revenues and profits in the energy sector. As a result, share prices of energy stocks tend to be highly correlated with oil prices. **Exhibit 4** shows the high correlation between the performance of the MSCI World Energy Index

Exhibit 3. Brent Oil vs. World GDP Growth

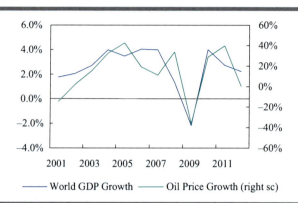

Sources: BP Statistical Review (2013) and FactSet database.

Exhibit 4. MSCI World Energy vs. Brent Oil

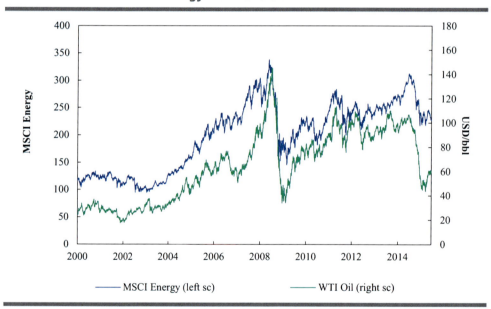

Sources: FactSet and Bloomberg.

and Brent oil prices. This index is a widely used benchmark that contains energy companies from all subindustries. Not surprisingly, the energy sector outperforms the broader MSCI World benchmark when oil prices are rising and underperforms the benchmark when oil prices are declining.

It should be noted that the MSCI World Energy Index does not represent all industry subsectors equally; it is highly dominated by IO companies (which make up about 53% of the total index) and E&P companies (about 22%). Oil services and drilling (14%), storage and transportation (6%) and R&M (5%) make up much smaller portions of this market-cap-weighted index. In addition, the index is highly focused on the developed markets—specifically, the United States (59%), the United Kingdom (16%), Canada (11%), France (5%) and Italy (3%)—whereas emerging markets currently reflect a rather small portion (7%) of the index's overall weight.

The high share of oil-producing companies (IO and E&P) in the MSCI World Energy Index explains the index's high correlation with oil prices because resource prices are a direct revenue and profit driver for these subsectors. Although I focus more on share price drivers for each subsector throughout this report, crude oil prices are a main share price driver for the energy sector as a whole. This observation is particularly important for investors who prefer to invest in broader energy benchmark indexes that are highly geared toward IO and E&P companies.

Appendix 1 describes several indicator prices that serve as relevant revenue, profit, and share price drivers for the energy sector. It provides average indicator prices for different types of crude oil, as well as natural gas along with complex refining margins and margins for kerosene products for the years 2000–2014.

GLOBAL ENERGY AND OIL DEMAND TRENDS

Because oil prices are highly dependent on future energy demand growth, the outlook for energy demand in general and for oil and gas demand in particular will affect the share price development of energy stocks. Therefore, I analyze some of the drivers for future energy demand growth and highlight long-term projections for energy demand trends that could have a profound impact on investor sentiment for the energy sector.

As I have pointed out, energy demand growth is highly dependent on global economic growth prospects. Global GDP is projected to grow at a long-term average of 2.5%–3.0% until 2035. Depending on which forecast service is used (e.g., the International Energy Agency, US Energy Information Administration, BP, ExxonMobil), total energy demand (including all fuels) is also forecast to reach compound annual growth rates (CAGRs) of 1.2%–1.7% between 2013 and 2035. The International Energy Agency (IEA) forecasts energy demand will grow at 1.2% per year from 2013 to 2035 and that energy demand will reach 17,387 Mtoe (million tonnes of oil equivalent) by 2035.

Because energy demand is projected to grow at a slower rate than overall economic activity, the global demand elasticity is less than 1. The world's energy intensity (energy required to produce one unit of GDP) is expected to decline over the long term as economies become more efficient in the use of energy in their manufacturing industries or simply require less energy as emerging economies transition from manufacturing to services industries.

In addition, the fuel mix (i.e., the relative share of each fuel in the energy demand pie) is also projected to change over the forecast period until 2035. Although oil is projected to remain the dominant fuel, its relative share is projected to decline from 31% in 2013 to 27% in 2035. Oil demand is forecast to grow at the slowest annual growth rate (0.5%) of any fuel between 2013 and 2035. This slow growth will cause it to lose market share relative to other fuels (similar to coal, which is forecast to grow by only 0.6%; its share is projected to decline from 29% to 25%).

In contrast, "cleaner" gas (in terms of reduced carbon dioxide emissions) is projected to gain market share; global gas demand is forecast to grow by 1.6% annually during this period, increasing its market share from 21% in 2013 to 24% in 2035. Demand for renewables and nuclear energy should have stronger average growth rates of 7.2% and 2.0%, respectively, but their relative shares in the global fuel mix are projected to remain low at 4% and 6%, respectively, by 2035. Considering that global oil demand is projected to grow at fairly benign rates (significantly below GDP growth), it is necessary to distinguish those regions where energy demand is still growing (emerging non-OECD economies) from developed (OECD) markets, where energy demand is expected to decline.

Oil demand in OECD countries (which have fewer energy-intensive and more service-oriented industries) is forecast to decline by 1.1% per year until 2035, and oil's share of their total energy demand is projected to decline from 50% in 2013 to 35% in 2035. Conversely, oil demand in developing non-OECD economies (which have energy-intensive and manufacturing-based growth models) is projected to increase by 1.6% per year until 2035, as shown in **Exhibit 5**. In 2013, for the first time, oil demand from non-OECD countries was larger than that of developed OECD countries. The share of non-OECD economies is projected to increase to 65% in 2035.

It is important to understand which industry sectors will drive future oil demand growth. Not only does the transportation sector generate the majority (72%) of global oil demand, but it is also the fastest-growing oil demand sector, albeit at a modest rate of a projected 1.6% per year until 2035, **Exhibit 6** shows.

As a result, transport's share of global oil demand will further increase to an estimated 79% by 2035. The industrial sector is forecast to post very small annual oil demand growth (0.2%). Demand in both the power sector (–2.7%) and the residential, commercial, and agricultural (RCA) sector (–0.8%) is projected to decline. With

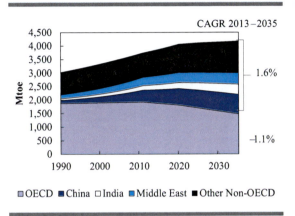

Exhibit 5. Global Oil Demand by Region

Source: International Energy Agency (2013).

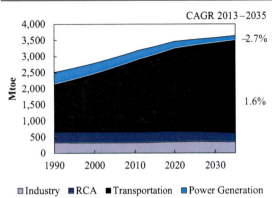

Exhibit 6. Global Oil Demand by Sector

Source: International Energy Agency (2013).

this sectorial oil demand split in mind, a strong increase in electric vehicles for road traffic would pose a serious threat to future oil demand growth (and to oil prices).

It is also important to highlight some global natural gas demand trends. Global gas demand is growing at 1.6% per year between 2013 and 2035, three times faster than global demand for oil or coal. Even OECD countries should show modest gas demand growth of 0.7% per year until 2035, whereas non-OECD gas demand is projected to reach average annual growth rates of 2.3% between 2013 and 2035.

Exhibit 7 shows significant gas demand growth coming from the Middle East, which increasingly wants to switch from oil-fired power generation to gas-fired turbines in coming years. Realizing this goal will help the region preserve oil as an important financing source, allowing it to generate higher oil export revenues, which can, in turn, be used to finance government budgets.

Although gas demand is projected to grow in each sector until 2035, industrial gas demand is expected to deliver the strongest growth rate (1.8%). Demand growth in the largest sector—power generation, which accounts for 50% of global gas demand, as shown in **Exhibit 8**—is forecast to increase at a healthy 1.5% per year; stricter environmental standards support operators switching from coal- and oil-fired power generation to cleaner gas-fired power plants. As a result, power generation will maintain the largest share at an estimated (50%) among all sectors until 2035; gas demand from power generation will grow in line with total global gas demand at 1.6% per year.

Exhibit 7. Global Gas Demand by Region

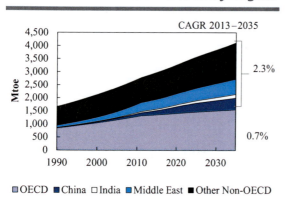

Source: International Energy Agency (2013).

Exhibit 8. Global Gas Demand by Sector

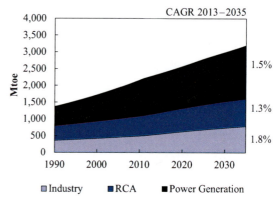

Source: International Energy Agency (2013).

OIL PRODUCERS: E&P AND IO COMPANIES

Oil producers need to establish a legal framework for any exploration work in a yet-unexplored basin in order to get the right to monetize a possible oil and gas discovery. Host governments auction leases for exploration acreage and invite interested oil and gas companies to submit bids for the acreage. These bids usually ask for an upfront fee and require that the company drills a certain number of wells within a specific time frame. The contractual duration of the lease depends on the country and the region but tends to last between 15 and 25 years and can be further extended. The lease agreement between the producer and the host government can take the form of either a production-sharing contract (PSC) or a tax and royalty concession.

Once the oil and gas company has secured the legal rights from the host government to explore for hydrocarbons, it hires a seismic company to conduct seismic surveys and imaging in the leased acreage from which potential drilling targets can be identified. After a potential oil and gas field has been chosen based on seismic analysis, the E&P company hires a drilling company and oil services providers to begin exploration and appraisal drilling of the field. The exploration and appraisal drilling cycle is highly correlated with oil price development but tends to track the underlying commodity price movement with a 12–15-month time lag—the time from the final investment decision to the drilling startup. Despite a significant improvement in seismic technology (from 2D to 4D imaging), the chances of discovering commercial oil and gas fields remain low (historically, below 20%).

OIL AND GAS PRODUCTION

Assuming an oil and gas discovery has been made, the oil and gas company has to develop the field in order to start production and commercialization. The development process (from discovery until peak production) can take 5–10 years, depending on the location (onshore or offshore) and the discovery's physical environment. During the development stage of the oil field's life cycle, development wells are drilled and oil services companies provide casing and completion support to construct the oil and gas well.

In addition, engineering and construction companies have to build the necessary infrastructure (such as offshore platforms, subsea pipelines, processing plants, and export terminals) to commercialize the oil and gas and to bring it to the market. Because the development phase for large oil and gas fields requires significant capital expenditure (capex) spending, the E&P company puts out tenders to E&C companies for front-end engineering and design (FEED) of the necessary infrastructure installations during the costly development stage, when E&P companies could be faced with significant cost overruns for larger projects.

Once the infrastructure development is completed and production of the oil and gas field has started, the production profile of individual producing wells determines how much oil and gas can ultimately be recovered from each well and from the whole field (sum of all wells). During the early stage of the production process, an exponential curve is fitted to the actual production data in order to extrapolate the production profile of an individual well (the type curve of the well).

Oil field production curves, as well as individual well curves, vary depending on geology and how they are developed and produced. Some fields have symmetric bell-shaped production profiles, but it is more common that the period of inclining production is briefer and steeper than the subsequent decline. More than half of a given well's production usually occurs after the related field has reached a peak or plateau. Once a field declines, its decline is typically exponential.

The projected cumulative production of a single well gives the E&P company an early estimate for the whole field's total reserves depending on how many wells the company intends to drill during the field's development. Oil and gas fields have different production profiles. Gas fields usually benefit from longer production plateaus but have steep decline rates, whereas oil wells tend to peak quickly, before the long terminal decline starts.

Once production enters the decline phase, E&P companies use different techniques to extend an oil and gas field's life and to increase the field's recovery factor (the portion of the recovered oil as a percentage of the estimated oil that is in place in the reservoir). So-called enhanced oil recovery (EOR) techniques are provided by oil services companies and include the injection of water, carbon dioxide, or chemicals into the well in order to enhance the oil flow and to improve the field's decline curve.

Large integrated oil companies tend to sell oil fields that have reached advanced decline phases and have become insignificant in terms of commercial value to the company. Smaller E&P companies buy these more depleted fields and apply EOR techniques to extend their production lives for several years. Often, the application of such techniques results in more oil being recovered from the well than was expected when the larger company sold its rights.

OIL AND GAS RESERVES

The Society of Petroleum Engineers (SPE) has been at the forefront of leadership in developing common standards for petroleum reserve definitions since the oil and gas industry recognized the need for a set of unified standard definitions that can be applied consistently by financial, regulatory, and reporting entities. Several industry bodies approved the publication of the current Petroleum Resources Management System (PRMS), which has been acknowledged as the oil and gas industry standard for referencing and categorizing petroleum reserves. It has also been used by the US SEC as a guide for its updated rules.[1]

PRMS provides the basis for classification and categorization of all petroleum reserves and resources and is based on an explicit distinction between (1) the development project that has been (or will be) implemented to recover petroleum from one or more accumulations and, in particular, the chance of commerciality of that project and (2) the range of uncertainty about petroleum quantities that are projected to be produced and sold in the future from that development project.

Each project is classified according to its maturity or status (broadly corresponding to its chance to achieve commerciality) using three main classes: reserves, contingent resources, and prospective resources. Separately, the range of uncertainty about the estimated recoverable sales quantities from that specific project is categorized based on the principle of capturing at least three estimates of the potential outcome—low, best, and high estimates—which reflect three specific scenarios as reserve outcomes from developing the project.

If the project satisfies all the criteria to be classified as reserves, the low, best, and high estimates are designated as proved (1P) reserves, proved plus probable (2P) reserves, and proved plus probable plus possible (3P) reserves, respectively. The equivalent terms for contingent resources are 1C, 2C, and 3C; the terms "low estimate," "best estimate," and "high estimate" are used in prospective resources.

The range of uncertainty relates to the uncertainty in the estimate of reserves (or resources) for a specific project. The full range of uncertainty extends from a minimum estimated reserve value for the project, through all potential outcomes, up to a maximum reserve value. If probabilistic methods are used to determine a reasonable range of high and low reserve estimates, the P90 (90% probability) and P10 (10% probability) outcomes are typically selected for the highest- and the lowest-volume estimates, respectively.

- Proved reserves: The P90, or 1P, reserve category gives a high degree of certainty (90% confidence) that these reserves can be recovered with relatively little risk. Proved reserves are further distinguished from proved developed reserves—reserves that can be recovered from existing wells with existing infrastructure and technology—and proved undeveloped reserves, which either include new undrilled wells or existing wells that require additional development activity and expenditure for recompletion.

---

[1] See www.sec.gov/rules/final/2008/33-8995.pdf.

- Proved plus probable reserves: The probabilistic equivalent to 2P reserves is the P50 reserve category, which implies that these reserves are less likely to be recovered than the 1P (or P90) reserve category. In probabilistic terms, there should be at least a 50% probability that the actual quantities recovered will be equal to or exceed the sum of estimated proved and probable reserves.

- Proved plus probable plus possible reserves: These 3P (or P10) reserves come with the highest degree of uncertainty; the developer ascribes only a 10% probability (that the actual quantities to be recovered will exceed the sum of proved, probable, and possible reserves). The 3P reserve measure is the least conservative reserve categorization; it includes possible reserves and assumes that 90% of the project's total reserves will be recovered. Thus, the 3P reserve measure will most likely overstate the total level of recoverable reserves.

Proved reserves get depleted every year by the amount of produced hydrocarbons from the existing reserve base. An important measure of success for oil-producing E&P and IO companies is how much of their proved reserves are replaced by hydrocarbon discoveries that increase the proved reserve base in the same year. An organic reserve replacement ratio of 100% indicates that all of the produced hydrocarbons were replaced in the same year by the same amount through an increase in newly discovered proved reserves (through own discoveries, not by acquiring reserves).

Whether oil and gas resources are technically and economically recoverable in order to be classified as proved reserves is highly dependent on the available technology and the level of oil and gas prices. As commodity prices increase, already discovered resources that were uneconomic to develop at depressed oil and gas prices may become economically recoverable and could then be reclassified as proved reserves. The opposite is true as well, and many high-cost resources may now lose their reserve status if they become uneconomic to develop after the steep oil price declines in 2014 and in 2015.

OIL SERVICES PROVIDERS

During the exploration, development, and production phases of an oil and gas field's life cycle, oil producers (E&P and IO companies) depend on the services provided by drilling, oil field equipment, and E&C companies. As an oil producer decides to explore a new field or to develop and produce a discovered field, the company has to rely on the specialized skills of these services companies. Thus, the business prospects of services suppliers depend on the capital spending plans of their oil- and gas-producing E&P and IO clients, which provide the revenue source for services companies.

Capital spending decisions of oil producers depend on the prospect of achieving a reasonable return from exploring or developing a new field, which is heavily influenced by commodity (i.e., oil and gas) prices and by the costs associated with drilling and with oil field services. Thus, during the strong oil price increase seen between 2003 and 2008, oil producers raised their capital spending budgets, only to cut them back in 2009 and 2010 and now again in 2014 and 2015, when oil prices declined sharply.

Commodity prices have a direct impact on the financial results of oil- and gas-producing E&P and IO companies, which explains the high correlation between commodity prices and capital spending decisions. Although the earnings prospects of service providers are *indirectly* linked to commodity prices (via the capital spending plans of their oil-producing clients), their share prices are also highly correlated with oil and gas price fluctuations (even though commodity prices do not *directly* affect their revenues).

Drilling companies provide rigs and operate them for their oil-producing clients on either a short-term or long-term contract basis. Onshore land drillers operate under different types of contracts, with drilling rates charged by the day or by the foot drilled or on a turnkey (all-inclusive) basis. Contracts for offshore drilling companies are mostly based on a day rate, but they occasionally contain turnkey contracts.

Oil field services companies provide the tools and services required to expedite the drilling of the well. These companies manufacture the necessary drilling support equipment or build it on the drilling site, maintain it during the drilling operation, and provide additional services, such as geological and seismic evaluations. E&C companies supply the necessary infrastructure to bring the produced hydrocarbons to the market.

The following sections describe the products and services provided by contract drilling, oil field services, and E&C companies in more detail.

CONTRACT DRILLING

Drilling companies can be categorized as onshore or offshore drillers.

OFFSHORE DRILLING COMPANIES

Offshore rigs are classified according to their maximum drilling depth, as shown in **Exhibit 9**: shallow coastal water (up to 500 feet), intermediate water (501–5,000 feet), deepwater (5,001–7,500 feet), and ultra deepwater (deeper than 7,501 feet). The deepest offshore drilling activity is currently taking place at about 10,000 feet, but the target hydrocarbon reservoir underneath the seabed could be as deep as 30,000 feet below the sea floor. Offshore rigs are also distinguished by their mechanism of support: from the bottom for a jack-up (which is connected by retractable legs to the sea floor) or from the water's surface by so-called floaters (i.e., semisubmersible or drill ship).

Offshore drilling rigs need to be distinguished from offshore production platforms, which float on the water's surface and are positioned above a group of producing wells. These platforms are usually owned by the oil- and gas-producing companies, not by the oil field services companies. The vessels are typically referred to as FPSOs (floating, production, storage, and offloading).

Exhibit 9. Categorizing Offshore Drilling Rigs

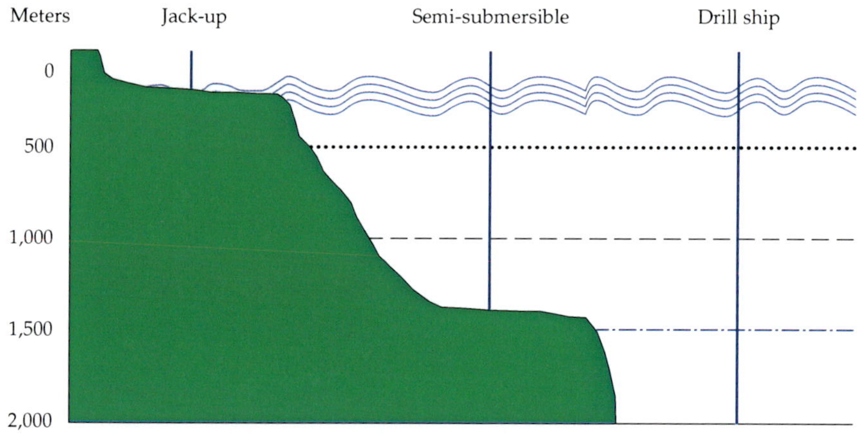

Source: Deutsche Bank (2013).

JACK-UP RIGS

Jack-up rigs operate in shallow water (i.e., less than 400–500 feet deep). These rigs are categorized according to their support system (mat supported versus independent leg supported) and based on the position of the drilling system on the rig (slot versus cantilever). Independent leg–supported jack-up rigs can have three legs on a triangular-shaped barge hull or four or more legs on rectangular hulls. Once the hull is positioned above the drilling site, the legs of the rig are lowered until they reach the ocean floor and are used to raise (i.e., "jack up") the hull above the height of the highest anticipated waves. When moved between drilling locations, the hull is towed by tugs and the legs stick out into the air.

SEMISUBMERSIBLE RIGS

Because semisubmersibles are not standing on legs, they are not limited to water depth of only 400 feet and thus can also drill in intermediate water and deepwater locations. Semisubmersibles have two or more air-filled steel floats (pontoons) to which the rig is connected, held in place by large anchors. With pontoons installed below the water's surface, semisubmersibles offer the very stable drilling platform required to drill in deep waters. A semisubmersible can be moved to a new drill site by towboats.

DRILL SHIPS

Drill ships are vessels similar to ships typically used for transportation. They tend to be used for exploration drilling in remote and very deep waters because they can drill while floating on the water's surface. The drilling takes place through a hole in the center of the ship's hull called the "moon pool," where a large derrick is permanently installed. Drill ships can drill holes up to 30,000 feet deep while operating in water depths up to 12,000 feet. Drill ships are very mobile; they can be easily and inexpensively moved between drilling locations.

Floating semisubmersibles and drill ships are much more unstable than jack-up rigs because they move with the waves and currents of the open water while the wellbore (a hole drilled to aid in the exploration and recovery of hydrocarbons) remains fixed in place. Many drill ships are equipped with dynamic positioning systems that enable the ship to maintain its location without anchoring by activating thrusters to keep the ship from straying too far from its location.

Transocean has the world's largest and most diverse fleet of offshore drilling rigs, which is almost equally split between shallow water jack-up rigs and floaters. Furthermore, as shown in **Exhibit 10**, Transocean has the largest number of ultra deepwater rigs in its fleet. Ensco, Rowan, and Hercules focus more on shallow water drilling; jack-up rigs make up the majority of their total fleet.

Exhibit 10. Fleet Composition of Major Offshore Drilling Companies

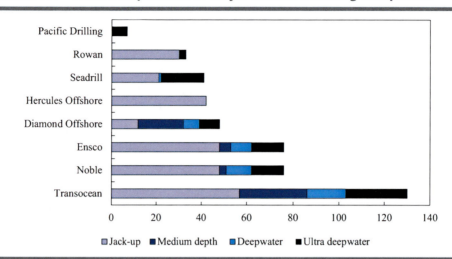

Source: Company information as of 2015.

The main revenue and profit driver for drilling companies is the price (day rate) that they can charge for rendering their drilling services to oil and gas producers. Day rates are directly determined by the utilization of specific rig types and the industry's overall supply and demand balance for certain rigs. As shown in **Exhibit 11** and **Exhibit 12**, the rig utilization for floaters has been a little higher and less volatile than for shallow water jack-up rigs over the past 10 years.

The discovery of new offshore hydrocarbon basins creates demand for new rigs. Such demand depends, however, on the oil price because the price affects the capex budgets of oil and gas producers for offshore exploration drilling activity. The development of new rigs depends on the availability of debt financing and the level of day rates that a drilling company expects to receive relative to the cost of buying or building a new rig.

The typical cost for a new jack-up rig is about $200 million, and the rig can be expected 18–30 months after the order is placed. Floaters are more expensive and cost about $600 million with a somewhat longer construction time of 24–36 months. Given the long lead times required to build new rigs, drilling companies must take a long-term view of the rig market and try to project the level of day rates for newbuild rigs over the next three to five years.

The main shipyards involved in building jack-up and floating rigs are Singapore-based Keppel Offshore & Marine and Sembcorp Marine as well as Samsung Heavy Industries and Hyundai Heavy Industries in South Korea. Lamprell, based in the United Arab Emirates, is an emerging player in the newbuild rig business; it has traditionally focused on refurbishing and upgrading existing fleets of older rigs operating in the Arabian Sea.

The day rates for floaters are significantly higher than for shallow water jack-up rigs. **Exhibit 13** and **Exhibit 14** provide examples of day rates for jack-up rigs versus floaters in the Gulf of Mexico. Given the increased technological requirements and costs of building deepwater rigs, floaters tend to have higher and more stable utilization rates than jack-up rigs; they are usually built to order for a committed buyer. In contrast, the commodity character of lower-tech jack-up rigs explains the greater volatility in day rates and lower fleet utilization compared with deepwater floaters in the Gulf of Mexico.

Exhibit 11. Global Jack-Up Supply and Demand

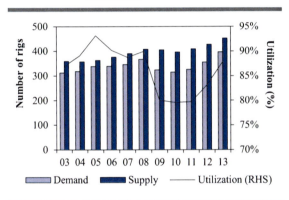

Source: IHS Petrodata (2013).

Exhibit 12. Global Floater Supply and Demand

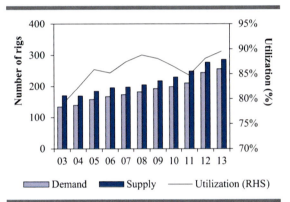

Source: IHS Petrodata (2013).

Exhibit 13. Gulf of Mexico Jack-Up Day Rates

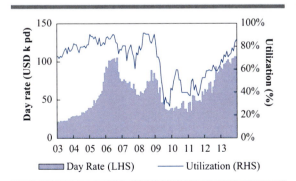

Source: IHS Petrodata (2013).

Exhibit 14. Gulf of Mexico Floater Day Rates

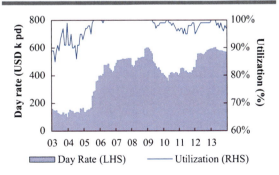

Source: IHS Petrodata (2013).

ONSHORE DRILLING COMPANIES

Similar to offshore rigs, land rigs are categorized by how deeply they can drill. Light-duty rigs drill to depths of up to 5,000 feet; medium-duty rigs, up to 10,000 feet; heavy-duty rigs, up to 16,000 feet; and very heavy-duty rigs can reach up to 30,000 feet. The drilling depth depends on the rig's horsepower (which determines how much weight the drill string, defined in the next section, can handle) and can be derived by multiplying the rig's horsepower (HP) by a factor of 10–12. Thus, it requires at least a 1,000 HP rig to drill a well with a target depth of 10,000 feet.

Land rigs can be further categorized as mechanical or electric-drive rigs, which use either AC (alternating current) or SCR (silicon-controlled rectifier) electric drives. Electrical rigs are more efficient than the older mechanical rigs. Mechanical rigs rotate the drill string with a rotary table, whereas electric-drive rigs use a top drive to rotate the drill string. During rotary drilling, a hollow pipe with a drill bit (explained in the next section) is rotated to cut the rock in the ground, and the weight of the pipe pushes the rotating drill bit further down. As the hole gets deeper, pipe is added so the drill bit can dig deeper.

According to the Baker Hughes Rig Count, there were 3,570 active rigs operating globally at the end of 2014.[2] The United States alone accounted for 1,882 rigs—53% of global drilling activity. Because oil prices have dropped severely since June 2014, the global rig count has also fallen by 47% over the past one and a half years, to 1,891 rigs in January 2016. The global rig count decline was driven by the US onshore market, where the number of rigs had fallen by 72% over the past one and a half years to 541 rigs in January 2016. Although the number of rigs drilling for gas in the United States has been in decline since 2009 (when US gas prices started to fall in response to rising US shale gas production), the number of oil rigs has also collapsed by 73% from the peak in September 2014, reaching 439 rigs in February 2016.

China and Russia are also large drilling markets but are not included in the Baker Hughes rig count because no official data are available.

DRILLING EQUIPMENT AND OPERATIONS

Drilling operations consist of repetitive processes, such as adding new joints of pipe as the hole deepens, hoisting the drill pipe out of the hole to replace the drill bit, and running it back to the bottom of the well. The drill string is an assembly of drill pipe and collars that extends from the rig floor to the bottom of the hole. A large-diameter steel pipe (or casing) is run into the hole and cemented at various predetermined intervals. Drill pipe connects the drilling rig at the surface with the drill bit at the

---

[2]The Baker Hughes Rig Count is an important business indicator for the drilling industry and its suppliers and a leading indicator for future oil production. Monthly Baker Hughes rig count data are provided in more detail in Appendix 3.

bottom of the well. The joints between sections of steel drill pipe are welded together to form the drill string. Drilling rigs have an inventory of 10,000–25,000 feet of drill pipe available, depending on their size and drilling depth.

The drill bit is a forged metal tool with sharp teeth that is positioned at the bottom of the drill pipe and rotates rapidly to penetrate the ground and dig the drilling hole into which the casing is laid to construct the well. There are different types of drill bits for different rock formations, and they can range in diameter from about 4 to 48 inches. The shape of the drill bit and the spacing of its cutting teeth are designed to maximize the penetration and the durability for a specific kind of rock.

Drilling fluids (or muds) have several functions during drilling operations. They lubricate and cool the rotating drill bit, remove cuttings of rock, and control pressure in the hole. Drilling fluids are mixtures of clays and chemicals that are custom blended to meet the specific conditions of a particular well. Drilling fluids are pumped into the wellbore through the drill pipe, and the mud exits the drill bit into the wellbore through the nozzles on the bit.

The flowing drilling mud removes rock cuttings from the drill bit and pushes them back up to the surface on the outside of the drill string in the space between the drill pipe and steel casing (the annulus). After the rock cuttings have been removed from the drilling fluid at the surface, the drilling mud is recycled and pumped back again into the wellbore.

Steel casing is used to line the drilled open hole from the drill bit in the drilling formation and to prevent the open wellbore from disintegrating or collapsing into the open hole. The well casing is then cemented into the drilled hole in order to prevent drilling fluids from migrating between formations.

After the well starts producing hydrocarbons, steel tubing, through which the oil and gas flows to the surface, is run into the well. Production tubing protects the wellbore casing from corrosion and the deposition of byproducts, such as sand. The steel tubing is about 5–10 centimeters in diameter and is stabilized inside the well casing with expandable packing devices.

Oil companies purchase the steel pipes, casing, and tubing directly from steel companies, not from oil field equipment providers. Depending on the steel price, the pipes, tubing, and casing equipment make up the second-largest expense item for an E&P company when drilling a well (after the drilling day rate paid to the drilling company for drilling the well).

Wellhead equipment is installed at the surface to provide the suspension point and pressure seals for the casing strings that run from the bottom of the hole to the surface pressure control equipment. While drilling the well, surface pressure control is provided by a blowout preventer (BOP). The BOP is a specialized valve developed to cope with extreme erratic pressures and uncontrolled hydrocarbon flow (formation kicks) during the drilling process. BOPs control the pressure in the wellbore and prevent the well pipe, casing, and tubing equipment from being blown out of the wellbore during the drilling process.

Once the well has been drilled and is producing, the surface pressure control is provided by wellhead equipment consisting of valves that are assembled with other components into a structure referred to as a "Christmas tree." The Christmas tree contains isolation valves and choke equipment that control the surface pressure and the flow of hydrocarbons from a producing well by forming a seal to prevent well fluids from leaking at the surface.

OIL FIELD SERVICES

During the drilling operations, oil field services companies offer a range of services, and many services companies are active in different segments. I categorize the wide range of oil field services into three areas: formation evaluation, completion and stimulation, and production and well maintenance.

FORMATION EVALUATION

Seismic imaging and analysis companies measure, process, and interpret geophysical data on land and underwater to help oil companies evaluate subsurface geology before the drilling process starts. Seismic imaging uses acoustic signals to determine the structure of underground geological formations and to map the layers of rock beneath the surface in order to detect the presence of hydrocarbon reservoirs and to decide on which areas to focus the drilling program. As seismic data are collected before the actual drilling program begins, the amount of seismic data analysis can be seen as an indicator of future drilling activity. Major seismic data companies are WesternGeco (a unit of Schlumberger), Compagnie Générale de Géophysique-Veritas (CGG), and Fugro.

After a potential hydrocarbon reservoir has been identified by seismic imaging and the drilling program has begun, the geological properties of the rock and the wellbore when the wells are drilled must be measured and recorded. This information helps the E&P company identify reservoir rocks and hydrocarbon pay zones along the drilled well.

Wireline logging (or well logging) is a data-recording device that provides a log, or test, to determine the makeup of the geological formation and the presence of hydrocarbons in the well. Electronic instruments are lowered into the well on a wireline (a strong, fine wire spooled onto a reel), which transmits the measured data to the surface to be recorded.

Two types of wireline services can be distinguished: First, open-hole wireline is used in wells without casing that have not been completed. Open-hole logs help to determine the location and reserve potential of hydrocarbons. Second, cased-hole wireline logging gathers additional data after the well has been completed about production data and mechanical services, including where to place the perforation in the casing to allow hydrocarbons to flow into the well.

Wireline logging has the disadvantage that drilling has to be stopped while the wireline tool is run down into the wellbore and back up again. Logging while drilling (LWD) or measurement while drilling (MWD) reduces the drilling downtime associated with wireline logging by incorporating measurement tools onto the drill bit. As a result, these tools can collect data during the drilling process without having to insert a separate wireline into the wellbore. LWD does not require a wireline because it transmits the data wirelessly to the surface.

The MWD tool is a collar that records drilling parameters at the drill bit. MWD measures the weight on the drill bit, the rate of penetration, and pump pressure during drilling without requiring a pause in the drilling process in order to run separate survey tools into the wellbore. Considering the time that is needed to pull several thousand feet of drill string from the wellbore, MWD provides a significant cost and time savings to wireline logging.

Directional drilling has improved the efficiency and accuracy of reservoir development together with the ability to log and measure data during drilling operations. During directional drilling, the top part of the well is drilled vertically down and then deflected at an angle so that the wellbore curves in the desired direction and the drill penetrates the reservoir laterally while special drilling tools and devices measure the direction and the angle of the wellbore.

In horizontal drilling, the operator deflects the well off the vertical axis to the point that it runs parallel to the surface. For some reservoirs, a single horizontal well is more effective than several vertical wells because the horizontal well allows recovery of a greater percentage of a formation's total hydrocarbon reserves. Horizontal drilling techniques are normally used to extract energy from a hydrocarbon source that itself runs horizontally, such as a layer of shale rock.

WELL COMPLETION, STIMULATION, AND PRODUCTION MAINTENANCE

The drilled well is completed and prepared for production by cementing a steel casing (metal tube) into the open wellbore to stabilize the drilling formation and to prevent the wellbore from collapsing. Oil services companies apply methods to stimulate the flow of hydrocarbons from the well, such as pressure pumping and hydraulic fracturing.

These techniques are very important for unconventional reservoirs (e.g., shale gas and shale oil) that are characterized by low porosity, and technological advancements in hydraulic fracturing together with horizontal drilling have made the development of unconventional shale reservoirs economic. After hydrocarbons begin to flow, production declines start to set in rather quickly, requiring further stimulation and artificial lifting services in addition to maintaining or replacing existing wellbore equipment (such as casing or tubing).

During well completion, cement is pumped down into the wellbore and then back up on the sides through the annular space between the casing and the wall of the wellbore. When the cement has hardened, it protects the outside of the steel casing against corrosion and helps stabilize the formation of the well.

Well stimulation includes acidizing and pressure pumping (i.e., hydraulic fracturing). Oil services companies pump pressurized acid or water into the well in order to create formations in the reservoir with paths through which hydrocarbons can flow from the formation into the well.

Hydraulic fracturing is the main pressure-pumping service; during the process, high-pressure fluid consisting of water, chemicals, and sands or artificial proppants is pumped into the wellbore in order to create small fractures in the rock formations. When the hydraulic pressure is removed from the wellbore, the small grains of sand or artificial proppants keep the small fractures open in the rock formation through which hydrocarbons can flow into the wellbore.

The strength and durability of these proppants (made of sand or porcelain) during the hydraulic fracturing process becomes more important at greater drilling depths, where pressure and stresses on formation fractures increase. The development of unconventional shale or tight reservoirs has become possible only through the development of hydraulic fracturing techniques.

Hydraulic fracturing faces strong political and environmental opposition in several countries as well as several US states. It is controversial because the pressurized drilling fluid contains chemicals (including benzene, methanol, ammonium bisulfite, and so forth) that, if not handled appropriately during the fracking process, could leak through the well and contaminate drinking water.

Well servicing is required for existing wells with routine maintenance services and wellbore modifications or repairs. Oil services companies provide special workover and well-servicing rigs for routine repair and maintenance requirements.

Artificial lift systems need to be installed to defer the natural production decline of a producing well; this mechanical pumping system compensates for a lack of sufficient reservoir pressure when lifting the hydrocarbons to the surface. If the pressure in the wellbore is below the reservoir pressure, hydrocarbons can flow from the reservoir to the wellbore. Reservoir pressure decreases as reservoirs get depleted, and the natural flow of hydrocarbons can thus fall below a profitable rate.

Although demand for artificial lifts typically increases as reservoirs age, an artificial lift is often required from the start of production in water-producing oil and gas wells. It is also sometimes used to increase the flow rate in naturally flowing wells. The total market value of the global artificial lift market is estimated to be about $8.0 billion.

Several artificial lift technologies are available. Rod pumps (also commonly known as pumpjacks) and electric submersible pumps (ESPs) together account for about 80% of the global artificial lift market; other technologies—such as hydraulic pumping systems, gas lift (in which gas is injected into the tubing), and progressing cavity pumps—make up the remainder.

Specialty chemicals are used to enhance the production of mature hydrocarbon wells and to extend the life of production equipment. Specialty chemicals help to achieve greater oil field efficiency while minimizing the impact on the environment.

The long history of US oil and gas exploration has its origins in Titusville, Pennsylvania, where the first oil well was drilled in 1859. Since then, the US oil industry has developed a highly competitive and technology-driven oil services industry. Thus, US oil services companies have also become global market leaders in all key service segments and continue to dominate several oil field services industries.

Exhibit 15 provides estimates about market shares and the industry positioning of the "Big Four" US oil services companies (soon to be "Big Three," assuming that Halliburton's proposed acquisition of Baker Hughes, which was announced in November 2014, closes).

Exhibit 15. Market Shares in the Oil Field Services Industry as of 2013

	Baker Hughes		Halliburton		Schlumberger		Weatherford	
	Position	Share	Position	Share	Position	Share	Position	Share
Seismic data			6	4%	1	24%		
Wireline logging	3	10%	2	20	1	42	4	5%
Logging while drilling	3	12	2	30	1	51	4	7
Directional drilling	3	17	2	22	1	32	4	8
Drilling fluids	3	11	2	24	1	38		
Drill bits	1	35	3	15	2	25		
Completion services	1	29	2	21	3	16	3	15
Pressure pumping	3	16	1	30	2	22	6	4
Artificial lift	3	14			2	17	1	28
Specialty chemicals	1	42			4	8	8	3

Source: Company information, Spears, and industry sources (2014).

ENGINEERING AND CONSTRUCTION

When oil has been discovered after exploration efforts, oil companies need to get the infrastructure and equipment in place to produce the hydrocarbons, to bring the produced oil and gas to the market (pipelines or liquefied natural gas, or LNG, terminals), or to convert raw hydrocarbons into refined oil products (gasoline) or derivatives (petrochemicals). Although most of the drilling-related exploration activities I have described take place underneath the ground's surface (or below the seafloor), the E&C activities described in this section are also connected with the development of hydrocarbon resources and mostly include above-ground or -seafloor) activities, such as laying pipes (onshore or offshore), building LNG terminals, constructing refineries, and developing petrochemical plants.

Just as the described oil field services companies provide drilling-related services below the surface for oil companies, E&C companies build the necessary infrastructure (pipelines, terminals, and refineries) for their clients. Together, oil field services and E&C companies constitute the broader oil services industry space, and the capital spending of their client companies (international oil companies, or IOCs, and E&P companies) represents the revenue base for the entire oil services sector. The capital spending related to drilling activities below the surface are usually categorized as exploration spending of oil producers, whereas capex for E&C activities above the surface fall under development spending.

Although some companies offer services related to both above- and below-surface and -seafloor activities, US services companies tend to focus on exploration-related drilling and completion services (pressure pumping, directional drilling, wireline logging, and so forth) below the surface. In contrast, their European peers offer primarily E&C activities when developing the field and installing the infrastructure to bring hydrocarbons to the market. European E&C companies participate in the reservoir's full life cycle—from the engineering, design, construction, and installation (including commissioning) of the oil and gas field's equipment.

EXPLORATION AND DEVELOPMENT CAPITAL EXPENDITURE

Global capex spending by IOCs, E&P companies, and national oil companies (NOCs) has recovered since the 2008–09 global financial crisis and reached an estimated $700 billion in 2014. E&C capex for the development of oil and gas reservoirs has always dominated global capex spending with an estimated share of about 70% of the total capex pie. Despite a significant capex decline during the 2008–09 financial crisis (14% contraction in 2009), global capex spending has increased on average by 9% per year since 2002. The recent oil price decline in 2014, however, will most likely trigger another contraction in global capex spending in 2015 (similar to in 2009).

Rising oil services costs for labor and materials have accounted for not only an increase in exploration and development activity in response to higher oil prices but also a large share of the increase in the total capital spending of oil and gas producers. Cost inflation has become an important issue for IOCs and E&P companies and is expected to curb their capex spending over the next few years. Meanwhile, the share of capex spending by less cost-sensitive NOCs has consistently increased over the past decade—from 35% in 2004 to an estimated 44% of global capex spending by 2014.

Capital spending for exploration and development services above and below the earth's surface or seafloor constitutes the order backlog in oil services companies—that is, the aggregate value of the company's already awarded projects at a specific point in time. As the projects reach completion, the oil services company realizes the related revenue and profit from the project and removes the project from the order backlog. Thus, the size of the order backlog drives the service company's future revenue potential; projects can have a shelf life ranging from three months to five years from start to completion.

ACCOUNTING FOR LONG-TERM CONTRACTS

Only E&C companies (mostly the European players) report an order backlog because the nature of their contracts is long term (i.e., three months to five years). In contrast, US oil field services companies do not report a backlog because most of their contracts related to subsurface exploration activities are very short term and they often book orders on a daily or weekly notice.

Two accounting methods are used to transform long-term contracts from the order backlog into revenues and, ultimately, profits. The basic revenue and profit realization principle for long-term contracts is the completed contract method, whereby the project's total value is converted into revenues upon the project's completion. Although project costs are expensed as they occur during the construction period, the profit will not be realized until the project is fully completed at the end of the construction phase; therefore, the completed contract method leads to very volatile earnings profiles.

Alternatively, the percentage of completion method can be used for revenue and profit recognition of long-term contracts when the project's progress toward completion can be measured on an annual basis. Under this accounting method, a portion of the project's total revenues is recognized every year based on the share of total costs that have been incurred so far. Thus, a proportional share of revenues and profits is recognized each year as the project advances toward completion, and the profit stream is less volatile under this accounting treatment.

For example, a $1 million project with estimated costs of $800,000 over a five-year construction period implies a 20% net margin. If the company incurred only

$100,000 of engineering costs during the first year of the project, then one-eighth of total revenues ($125,000) can be booked in the first year, and a net profit of $25,000 is recognized at the end of the first year ($125,000 less $100,000).

One of the biggest risks for E&C companies is the potential for cost overruns during the construction phase, when the projects are still in the company's order backlog. If costs increase unexpectedly before the completion of the project, the anticipated margins of the order backlog become too high because the realized margins will be lower than previously projected.

Considering that project costs significantly increased over the decade before the 2008–09 financial crisis because of rising labor and material costs, as well as an increase in subcontracted services costs, several E&C companies (e.g., Saipem, Technip) have had to issue profit warnings in recent years related to cost overruns (or overly optimistic margin expectations for their order backlogs).

TYPES OF LONG-TERM CONTRACTS

Long-term contracts can be categorized into three types.

LUMP-SUM CONTRACTS

In a lump-sum contract, the client of the oil services company pays a fixed price for the completion of the entire project (including engineering, procurement, construction, and installation services), and the project's execution risk lies entirely with the contractor (i.e., E&C company). If unforeseen cost increases occur during the construction phase that were not budgeted in the original contract price, the liability lies with the E&C company, and its profit margin for the project declines (unless a change in the project's scope accounts for the cost increase).

Thus, lump-sum contracts should always include an additional buffer in the form of a cost contingency of up to 15% of the project's price to account for execution risks relating to rising subcontracting costs. If all goes well and cost overruns during the project execution can be avoided, the contingency increases the E&C company's profit margin. If not, the cost contingency protects the contractor's profit margin unless the cost overruns exceed the cost contingency.

COST PLUS CONTRACTS

Under cost plus contracts, E&C companies can recover from their clients any cost increases that occur during the project execution phase (for expenses related to materials, labor, equipment, and subcontractor services). In contrast to lump-sum contracts, in a cost plus contract, the client bears the risk of cost inflation. The project price is split into a cost recovery amount and an additional profit fee, which can be a fixed or variable amount.

Under variable profit contracts, the profit fee can be set as a percentage of the recoverable costs or as an incentive-based fee, which increases if well-defined performance metrics (delivery times, operating efficiencies, or cost savings targets) are met or exceeded. Because cost plus contracts favor E&C companies in terms of execution risk, E&P clients tend to set strict performance and execution standards to reduce additional costs and to detect defects during the development phase.

Many E&C companies have switched their long-term project contracts from lump-sum to cost plus contracts because the latter allows them to pass on cost increases during the project completion to their E&P customers. As a result, the share of cost plus contracts increased from about 26% of all contracts signed in 2005 to about 35% in 2012.

UNIT PRICE CONTRACTS

A combination of the previous two types of contracts, unit price contracts start as a cost plus arrangement during the procurement phase, when all subcontractors are selected and the recoverable cost amount for all procured services are defined. Beyond the recoverable costs associated with the procurement phase, the E&P client pays a fixed price for the entire project's completion (construction and installation). Thus, unit price contracts separate the total costs associated with the procurement phase from the overall costs for constructing and installing the entire project. The E&P client retains the cost risk during the procurement phase, and the E&C company has to manage the execution and performance risk during the later construction and installation phases.

REFINING AND MARKETING

THE REFINING PROCESS

Refining is the process of converting different grades of crude oil into finished products, such as gasoline or heating oil, by separating hydrocarbons with carbon chains of various lengths. The technological configuration of the refinery (whether it is a simple or complex refinery) and the type of crude oil that is processed as a feedstock in the refinery determine the product (the refinery's product yield or slate) output—the proportion of different refined products produced from one barrel of crude oil.

Crude oil can be classified as heavy or light crudes in terms of API (American Petroleum Institute) gravity, which is a measure of how heavy or light a crude oil is compared with water. The API gravity is derived from a formula that takes into account the crude oil's relative density to water and is scaled between values of 10 and 70. The higher the API gravity of a crude oil, the lighter it is. Light crudes have an API gravity above 35, whereas the gravity of heavy crude oils falls between 10 and 35. Light crudes contain fewer long-chain carbon molecules and have a lower viscosity (resistance to flow) than heavy crudes.

Crude oil is also categorized according to its sulfur content. Sweet crudes contain less than 0.7% sulfur, whereas sour crude grades have sulfur contents between 1.5% and 3.5%. Sweet crude grades with lower sulfur content are more valuable to refiners because they require less processing equipment and correspondingly lower capital investment in the refinery to convert it into refined products; sour crude oils require additional processing in order to meet regulatory specifications.

Exhibit 16 categorizes the most important internationally produced crude oils according to API gravity and sulfur content, and **Exhibit 17** shows the quality split of global oil reserves.

Appendices 1 and 2 summarize the average prices on an annual and quarterly basis between 2005 and 2014 for several crude oil grades shown in Exhibit 2.

Different crude oil qualities (light sweet, medium sour, and heavy sour) used as refinery feedstock yield different proportions of refined products. Thus, a refinery's product slate—that is, its product yield—reflects the technical configuration of a specific refinery (whether simple or complex) and the type of crude oil that is processed in the refinery (because crude oils differ in their hydrocarbon composition).

Exhibit 18 illustrates the typical product yield in a simple refinery for different crude oil feedstock qualities (light sweet, medium sour, and heavy sour crude) when the crude oil is heated and thereby physically separated into different groups

Refining and Marketing

Exhibit 16. Crude Oil by API Gravity and Sulfur Content

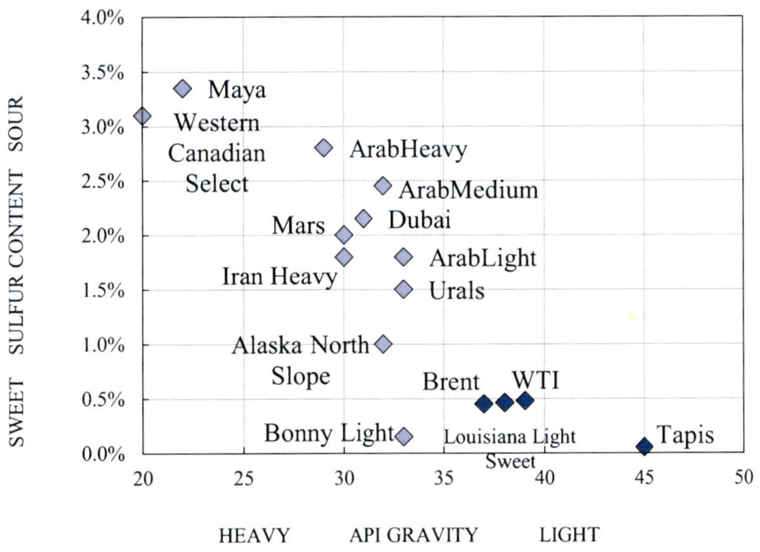

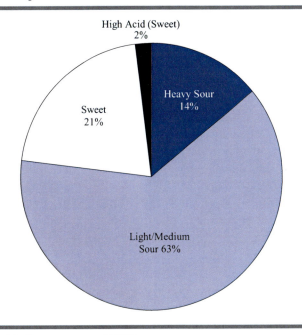

Sources: Valero, US Department of Energy, and industry reports.

Exhibit 17. Quality of Oil Reserves

- High Acid (Sweet) 2%
- Heavy Sour 14%
- Sweet 21%
- Light/Medium Sour 63%

Sources: Valero and industry reports (2013).

CFA Institute Industry Guides

Exhibit 18. Typical Product Yields from Different Crude Oil Feedstock Qualities

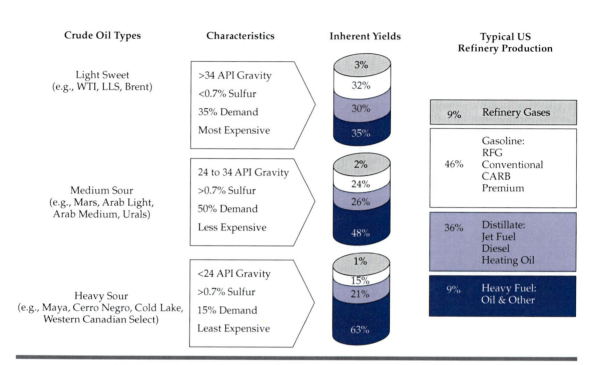

Sources: Valero and US Energy Information Administration (EIA) refiner production (2013).

of hydrocarbons. Without any conversion or additional processing, light sweet crude yields the highest portion of gasoline and distillates, which also make up the largest share of refined products in the United States.

After various hydrocarbon components are separated by boiling the crude oil at different temperatures in the refinery's distillation unit, various intermediate products can be further processed into several final product streams. This additional processing requires additional equipment in the refinery, which gives the refinery a higher level of complexity, as shown in **Exhibit 19**.

Heating crude oil to different boiling points in the distillation tower or vacuum unit yields several hydrocarbon components as intermediate or final products. These oil products can be distinguished by the length of their hydrocarbon chains and by their physical state (whether they are gaseous, liquid, or solid).

Refining and Marketing

Exhibit 19. Product Yield from the Refinery Distillation Process

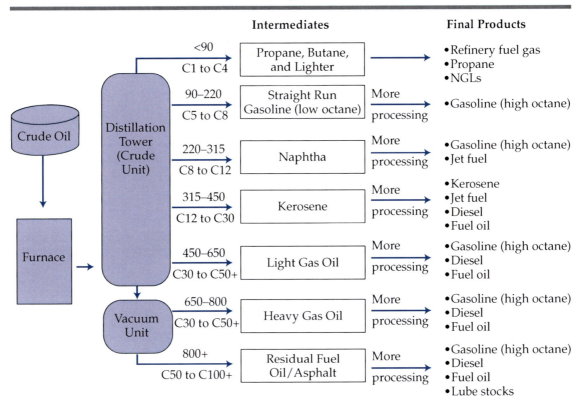

Source: Valero (2013).

- Petroleum gas is the lightest hydrocarbon chain, consisting of methane (known as C1, as it consists only of 1 carbon atom), ethane (C2), propane (C3), and butane (C4). At room temperature, it is in a gaseous state, but it can be vaporized and is mostly used for heating and cooking and as a feedstock for plastics. Petroleum gas can be liquefied under pressure and converted into liquefied petroleum gas (LPG) to be transported by pipeline and stored in tanks or large bottles.

- Naphtha is a light and clear liquid. As an intermediate product, it can be further processed into gasoline and jet fuel. As a final product, it is used as feedstock in the petrochemical industry in Europe and Asia and as a solvent in dry cleaning fluids and paint solvents.

- Gasoline is a motor fuel and is rated by its octane number, which is an index of quality that reflects the ability of the fuel to resist detonation and burn evenly under high pressure and temperatures inside the engine. It was common to add a form of lead to the cheaper grades of gasoline to increase the octane level before stricter environmental regulation was introduced to reduce carbon dioxide emissions. Now, aromatics and oxygenates are used in further processing to raise octane levels, and cars are equipped with catalytic converters that oxidize unreacted gasoline.

- Kerosene is a liquid fuel used for jet engines or as an intermediate fuel to be converted into diesel or fuel oil. Gas oil and diesel are other liquids used for automotive fuel and home heating oil. Both can be further processed into other products.

- Lubricating oil is a liquid fuel that is used to make motor oil, grease, and other lubricants. It does not vaporize at room temperature, but it is processed into various thicknesses—very light fuel, motor oil, gear oils, and semi-solid greases.

- Heavy gas oil, or fuel oil, is a liquid fuel used as a fuel in industrial sectors and to generate heat for power generation. As an intermediate product, it can be further processed into gasoline or diesel. Heavy grades of fuel oil are also used as bunker oil to fuel ships. When burned, heavy gas oil is the most polluting of all oil product components. Residual fuel oil has a solid state, such as coke, asphalt, tar, and waxes. These products are generally the lowest value of the crude barrel but can also be used as intermediates and processed into other products.

SIMPLE REFINERY

During the distillation or fractionation process in a refinery (also called "topping" or "skimming"), crude oil is separated into groups of hydrocarbon compounds with different boiling point ranges called "fractions" or "cuts." The size of the carbon chains (the number of carbon atoms) determines the boiling point ranges of different products in crude oil, with longer carbon chains requiring higher boiling points. Two distillation processes can be distinguished.

First, in atmospheric distillation, crude oil is heated to 350–400 degrees Celsius under atmospheric pressure. The liquid components fall to the bottom, vaporize through the distillation tower, and pass through several perforated trays (sieves). The lighter crude oil components, such as LPG, naphtha, and so-called straight-run gasoline are recovered at the lowest temperatures at the top of the tower. Then, middle distillates (jet fuel, kerosene, heating oil, and diesel fuel) fall below that.

Finally, the heaviest products (residuum or residual fuel oil) are recovered at the bottom of the atmospheric distillation unit (ADU).

Second, in a vacuum distillation unit, heavy distillates are separated from the residue of the first distillation process in a second distillation column under vacuum conditions. Vacuum distillation allows heavy hydrocarbons with higher boiling points—450°C and above—to be separated without getting cracked (i.e., broken down) into unwanted products, such as coke. Because there is less pressure in the vacuum unit (compared with atmospheric pressure in the ADU), several types of gas oil products that are slightly heavier than middle distillates can vaporize without being cracked or broken down further (which would be the case in the cracking process of a complex refinery as described in the next section).

Without any additional processing in the refining process, the skimming process of light sweet crude in a simple refinery yields the product slate shown in **Exhibit 20**.

Exhibit 20. Hydroskimming/Topping Process in a Simple Refinery

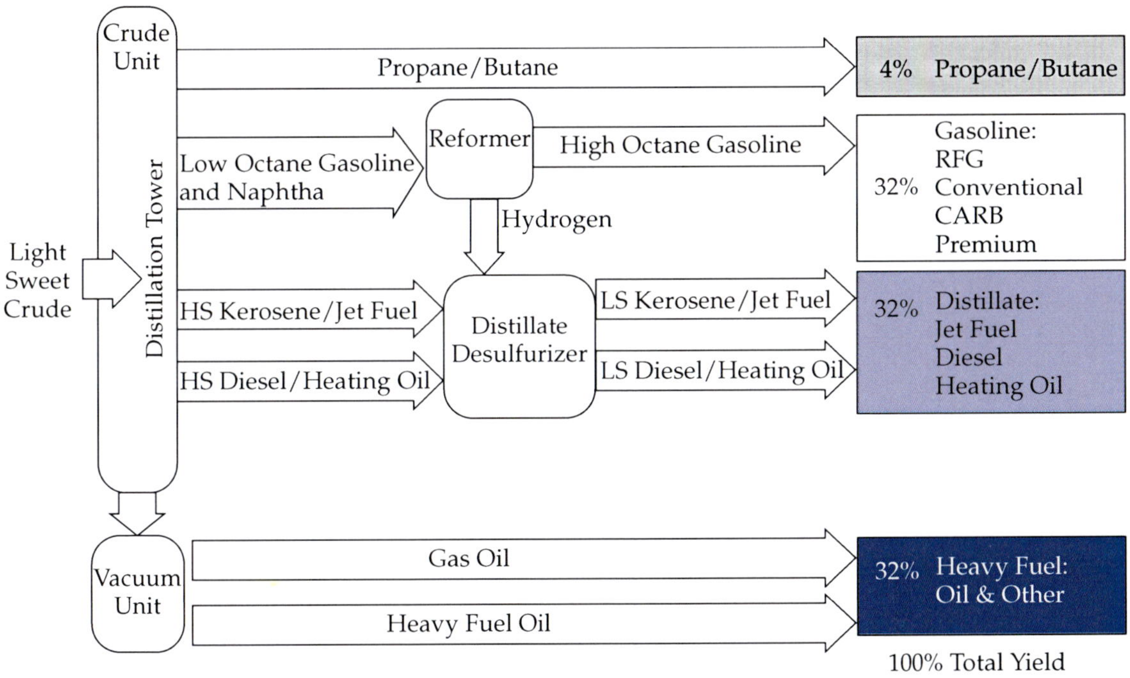

Source: Valero (2013).

COMPLEX REFINERY

The pure distillation process in a simple refinery does not alter the chemical structure of the hydrocarbon feedstock (light, medium, or heavy crudes). In contrast, the application of several conversion (or upgrading) processes in complex refineries alters the hydrocarbon's chemical structure by further treating and converting the intermediate product output from the initial distillation process into higher-value final products.

As a result, for the same barrel of crude oil feedstock, the refined product mix (yield) in a complex refinery can be altered by applying special conversion processes when compared with the product mix (yield) in a simple refinery. Thus, the conversion process in a complex refinery allows refiners to match their final oil product output more closely with the demand requirements in a specific market (or country).

The conversion processes in a complex refinery break down (crack) heavier hydrocarbon molecules of intermediate products with higher boiling points into lighter products (e.g., gasoline and diesel). Two main types of cracking processes can be distinguished—thermal cracking (using heat) and catalytic cracking (using chemical catalysts).

In thermal cracking, heavy intermediate products are heated under high pressure and thereby split into lighter hydrocarbon components. Coking is a special form of thermal cracking in which the heaviest intermediate output (i.e., heavy fuel oil) is converted into lighter petroleum products. Steam cracking and visbreaking are other forms of thermal cracking.

In catalytic cracking, heavy distillates are further broken down by a chemical reaction triggered by a chemical catalyst under controlled pressure and heat (450°C–500°C). Hydrocracking is a form of catalytic cracking that uses hydrogen as a catalyst in the conversion process. Fluid catalytic cracking uses a fine powder in a fluid state as a catalyst to vaporize the intermediate product during the cracking process.

The conversion process in a complex refinery changes (improves) the product yield for a specific crude oil feedstock. Although the distillation process in a simple refinery yields 48%–63% of lower-value heavy fuel oil from a barrel of medium or heavy sour crude oil (see Exhibit 18), the conversion process in a complex refinery reduces the share of heavy fuel oil in the final product mix to 15% and increases the total share of light and higher-value gasoline and diesel to 86% in the final product mix, as shown in **Exhibit 21**.

Exhibit 21. Conversion Process in a Complex Refinery

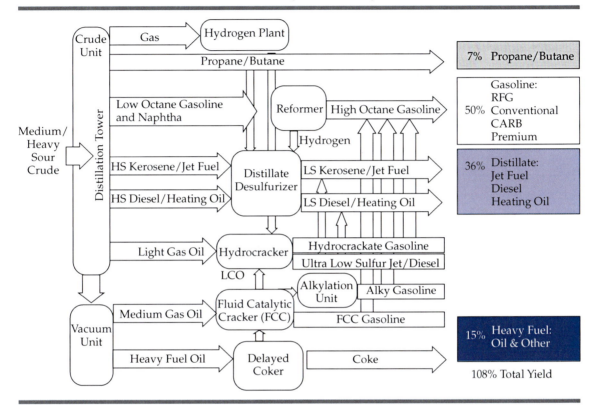

Source: Valero (2013).

REFINERY CONFIGURATION DRIVES REFINING PROFITS

The ability of a complex refinery to choose a cheaper medium or sour heavy crude oil as a feedstock and to convert it into higher-priced gasoline or middle distillate products (jet fuel, diesel, and heating oil) increases the profitability of complex refiners compared with simple refineries, which are less flexible in terms of feedstock choice and refined product output. Thus, a refinery's configuration or complexity has a significant impact on its profitability; more complexity increases the refiner's flexibility regarding feedstock choice and product slate.

FEEDSTOCK FLEXIBILITY

Complex refineries have more flexibility regarding the feedstock choice (light sweet and/or heavy sour), whereas simple refineries are more dependent on light sweet crude as a feedstock. Thus, complex refineries can benefit from pricing differences between higher-priced light sweet crude (WTI, Brent) and lower-priced heavy crudes (such as Russian Export Blend Crude Oil, known as Urals oil, and Mexican Maya Crude Oil, which tend to sell at a price discount that should theoretically reflect the value differential between product slates derived from the processing of sweet crude and those derived from heavy crude feedstock in a simple refinery).

In addition to benefiting from this heavy–light price spread, complex refiners gain from the greater flexibility of processing a wider range of light or heavy crude oils because they can capture temporary pricing differences between different types of heavy crudes (Urals versus Maya) or between different light crudes (such as the widening Brent–WTI price spread in 2011 and 2012; see Appendices 1 and 2).

The global refining system is still equipped to process mostly light sweet crudes. Therefore, when light sweet crude supply is constrained or product demand is high, refiners that are unable to process heavier or sour crudes have to compete for light sweet feedstock. As a result, the price premium for light versus heavy crudes widens to reflect the supply shortage for light sweet crudes. The premium can then exceed the normal price spread that should merely reflect the (theoretical) difference between product yields and processing costs inherent in light and heavy crude types. Thus, during times of high oil prices, complex refiners benefit from the additional feedstock price spread because they can use cheaper-than-normal heavy crudes as feedstock.

FLEXIBLE PRODUCT YIELD

Simple refineries have less flexible product yields (i.e., less choice to influence the share of higher-priced gasoline versus lower-priced fuel oil in their product mix) because they lack the necessary conversion units (called "crackers"). As complex refineries add conversion units, they are able to produce a product slate that includes a larger share of higher-priced fuel outputs, such as LPG, light distillates (gasoline and naphtha), and middle distillates (diesel, kerosene, and heating oil). Accordingly, they are able to reduce the share of lower-priced heavy fuel oil in their product mix because fuel oil is widely used in the power generation sector; therefore, the selling price of fuel oil in the power sector is constrained by low-cost fuel substitutes, such as coal and natural gas.

Thus, complex refiners benefit not only during times of high oil prices from a widening light–heavy crude oil price spread for their feedstock but also, when oil prices increase, on the product side. The economics of converting heavy fuel oil into gasoline improves when oil prices increase because their price differential (crack

Refining and Marketing

spread) widens as well. When oil prices increase, the price for transportation fuels (light distillate gasoline as well as middle distillate diesel and jet kerosene) increases almost proportionally with the rising feedstock price for crude oil because there are no effective substitutes for these transportation fuels.

In contrast, rising crude oil prices cannot be passed on by increasing the price for heavy fuel oil to power generation companies because heavy fuel oil can be substituted with cheaper coal or gas as alternative fuels in the power sector. Thus, while the upside price potential for heavy fuel oil is capped (by lower prices of substitutes), prices for light transportation fuels can continue to increase and the light–heavy price differential (crack spread) is widening in a high–oil price environment.

Exhibit 22 provides an example of the conversion margin between gasoline (as a light distillate) and heavy fuel oil at different oil price levels. The conversion margin widens as oil prices rise until gasoline demand starts to decline at gasoline prices above $4 per gallon—when so-called demand destruction starts to kick in—thereby limiting the upside potential for gasoline prices even if oil prices continue to increase.

Thus, a refinery's complexity is not defined only by its ability to use heavy sour crude oil as a feedstock because many complex refineries cannot process heavy crude oil. Instead, a refinery's complexity level depends on both its feedstock flexibility and its capability to convert lower-value products (e.g., heavy fuel oil) into higher-value oil products (e.g., gasoline and diesel) in order to capture the conversion premium.

Exhibit 22. Crack Spread Widens at Higher Oil Prices

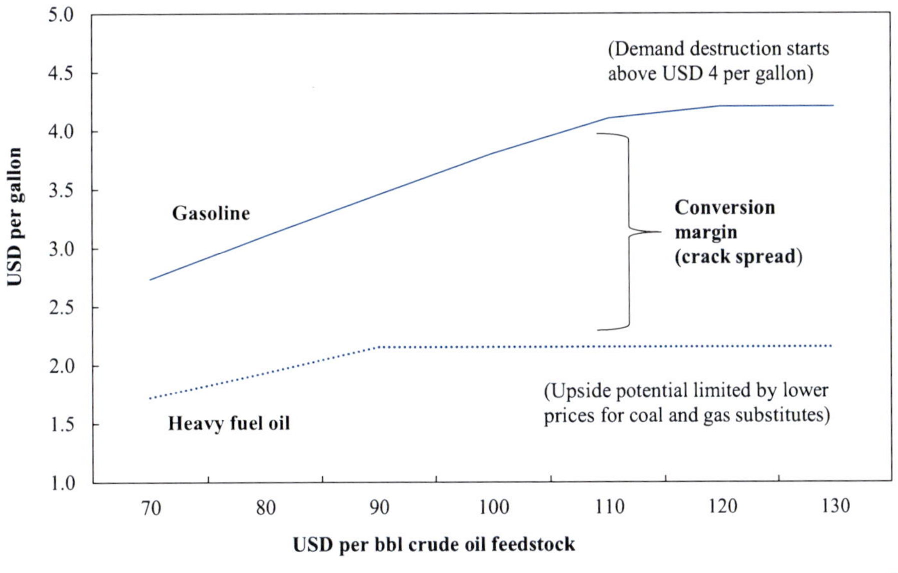

Sources: IEA and author's estimates.

NELSON COMPLEXITY INDEX

A refinery's complexity level is determined by the Nelson complexity index (NCI), which measures the refinery's secondary conversion (cracking or coking) capacity relative to the size of its primary distillation (skimming or topping) capacity. Each conversion unit in the refinery gets a complexity number assigned, which includes two for hydroskimming, five for cracking units, and nine for coking refineries.

The NCI for the whole refinery is then calculated as the capacity-weighted sum of all unit complexities relative to its crude distillation capacity, as shown in **Exhibit 23**.

Considering the advantages complex refineries have thanks to their feedstock flexibility and high-value oil product output compared with simple refineries, the obvious question is, Why do all refining companies not strive to run complex refineries? The reason is that upgrading the refining process requires additional capital

Exhibit 23. Calculation of the Nelson Complexity Index

Refinery Units	Processes	Capacity (kbd)	Nelson Complexity	Capacity-Weighted Complexity
Crude distillation unit (CDU) for topping and skimming	Crude oil separated into petroleum products by atmospheric distillation; naphtha produced but no gasoline	600	1	600
Hydroskimming	Atmospheric distillation, naphtha reforming, and desulfurization process to run light sweet crude and produce gasoline	250	2	500
Cracking	Vacuum distillation and catalytic cracking process added to run light sour crude to produce light and middle distillates	200	5	1,000
Coking	Coking unit added to run medium sour crude oil	100	9	900
Total		1,150		3,000
NCI for whole refinery				5.0

Note: kbd is thousand barrels per day.
Sources: Reliance Industries and author's calculations.

investment. Such expenditures might not lead to a similar improvement in the return on capital employed (ROCE) because additional capital costs outweigh the incremental profit margin.

If the refinery invests in upgrading conversion units to increase the output for specific oil products with depressed prices because the local market is in surplus, the additional capital and maintenance cost for added equipment could even reduce the return on the investment. Thus, the choice between a simple and a complex refinery is highly dependent on the product prices that can be achieved for a refinery's total product stream in specific markets. In some locations, less complex refineries with lower cash costs could be more profitable.

Feedstock availability is another factor to take into consideration when deciding whether to invest in a simple or a complex refinery (i.e., whether heavy or light crude is most readily available). Because US refiners can easily obtain heavy crudes from Canada and Venezuela, there are more complex refineries in the United States.

The NCI factors range from 1 (distillation process only) to 17 (most processing equipment upgrades). For US refineries, the average NCI is 10.4; about 75% of US refineries reach complexity levels between 7 and 13. In contrast, about 75% of West European refineries have an NCI between 6 and 10; therefore, the average complexity level of a West European refinery, with an average NCI of 8.2, is lower than in the United States, as shown in **Exhibit 24**.

In a global context, however, the complexity levels of North American and European refineries are the highest, closely followed by refineries in Asia Pacific (with an average NCI of 7.8). Refineries in the Middle East and in Africa have, on average, the lowest complexity level with average NCIs of 4.5 (see **Exhibit 25**).

Exhibit 24. NCI of US and European Refineries

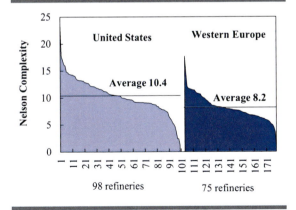

Source: Company information (2013).

Exhibit 25. Average NCI for Different Regions

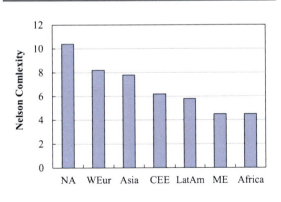

Source: Company information (2013).

REGIONAL PRODUCT BALANCES

Through investment in conversion units, refiners are able to adjust the specific product mix in order to meet demand for the different product streams in specific markets. It is not possible, however, to perfectly match the output from the refinery with the demands of the local regional market; product imbalances are frequently evident in regional refining markets. These product imbalances together with regulatory restrictions and fuel specifications can also affect refiners' profitability in different markets.

To the extent that a local market is short a particular product, refiners will be able to charge a premium for that product. This price premium is equal to the transport cost for an external supply source. Similarly, when there is excess supply of a specific product, the refiner may reduce prices to encourage sales or incur the transport cost for exporting the surplus. Although refining markets may be tight for specific products in certain regions, product flows ensure that tightness in any one regional market is not sustained and that, globally, the refining market for any product is not short of supply.

The US market remains tight across most major product categories but in particular for gasoline and jet fuel, for which it is dependent on imports. US refiners have increased their gasoline exports to South American countries since 2010, but the United States remains a net importer of gasoline products. The majority of the US car fleet is fueled by gasoline rather than diesel. Because US authorities are unlikely to sanction the building of a new grassroots refinery in the US market for environmental reasons, capacity growth is likely to be modest and will depend on the refining industry's ability to manage the bottleneck problem in existing plants. Thus, in the absence of a major deterioration in US gasoline demand, investors can expect US margins to be higher on average than margins in other geographic regions.

In contrast, the European market is significantly long gasoline, has some surplus fuel oil, and is export dependent for these two products. Given the maturity of Europe's gasoline demand owing to its more widespread use of diesel-fueled cars, European demand growth for gasoline is likely to be modest. With the exception of fuel oil, these imbalances are more likely to increase than to subside. Overall, European gasoline margins tend to be lower than those in the United States—something that is unlikely to change.

In contrast, Europe likely will be increasingly short diesel and gas oil products, whereas the growing surplus in the US market for these products means that Europe should be a key export market for US diesel and gas oil producers in coming years. Because Asia is expected to see an increasing deficit in fuel oil, Europe—as a surplus region for fuel oil—should continue to be a significant net exporter of fuel oil products to Asia.

REFINING MARGINS

Daily oil price movements are an indicator of upstream profitability, and refining margins provide a guide to the health of downstream returns. These volatile margins are merely the reflection of daily crude and oil product prices from a basket of oil products. They represent the incremental revenue that a refiner can generate from turning a barrel of crude into a basket of refined products, thereby reflecting the gross refining profit before taking a refinery's specific operating costs into consideration.

Because crude oil and oil product prices are readily available in most of the world's major regions, it is possible to calculate the gross refining profit or margin a refiner is likely to achieve on any given day. Indeed, several newswires (e.g., Reuters, Bloomberg) and oil agencies (e.g., Platts) publish daily or weekly gross margins for the major regional refining centers—namely, the US Gulf Coast, Northwest Europe (or Amsterdam, Rotterdam, Antwerp—known as ARA), and Singapore.

These "indicator" margins depict the gross margin per barrel that a regional refiner is likely to achieve when operating either a simple or complex refinery and using the crude oil that is widely processed in the region. Although these published margins are only price indicators—all refineries have different processing units with different cost structures—they do provide a good signal for refining profitability at any point in time and reveal the general margin trend in a specific region.

When calculating these indicator margins, simple assumptions are made about the local refinery's output. For example, the most commonly quoted refining margin, the Gulf Coast 3:2:1, assumes that for three barrels of oil, two barrels of gasoline and one barrel of low-value, heavy fuel oil are produced (put differently, one barrel of crude converts into 0.67 barrels of gasoline and 0.33 barrels of fuel oil).

Based on known crude oil and product prices, it is easy to calculate the gross refining margin: If the price of crude oil is $90/barrel and the wholesale prices for gasoline and fuel oil are $2.90/gallon and $1.50/gallon, respectively, the calculation of the refining margin is as follows (there are 42 gallons in a barrel):

0.67×1 barrel of gasoline $+ 0.33 \times 1$ barrel of fuel oil $- 1$ barrel of crude oil, or

$[(0.67 \times 2.9 \times 42) + (0.33 \times 1.5 \times 42)] - \$90 = (\$81.61 + \$20.79) - \$90 = \$12.40/bbl$

Other refining margins can be used to reflect the refining complexity of a specific refinery or region. For example, where light crude is refined and there is higher demand for heating oil, the appropriate margin ratio may be 2:1:1. Similarly, a refinery that yields significant amounts of heating oil and fuel oil might be 6:3:2:1 (with six barrels of crude oil yielding gasoline, heating oil, and fuel oil).

Refining margins are usually analyzed over several years to examine the price range over a given time period (10 or 15 years) and to detect seasonal trends within each year (higher margins during the summer months when gasoline demand peaks). Appendices 1 and 2 summarize the average complex 3:2:1 refining margins in the United States and in northwest Europe on an annual and quarterly basis between 2000 and 2014.

Product crack spreads calculate, in addition to indicator refining margins, the relative value between two refined products. The gasoline and diesel cracks reflect the conversion value in US dollars per gallon when refining a gallon of less valuable fuel oil or heating oil into higher-priced gasoline or diesel, respectively.

Refining margins reflect the price differential between crude oil as the feedstock in the refining process and the product prices for the refined product stream (gasoline, diesel, heating oil, and so forth). Thus, the underlying supply and demand balance for a specific product in a certain market is the main driver for the product price and thus for the refining margin for this product.

Demand for specific oil products is affected by efficiency gains (more fuel-efficient vehicles or power plants require less fuel), seasonality (more gasoline demand during the summer driving season and stronger heating oil demand during the winter heating season) and interfuel substitution (fuel oil competes in power markets with gas and coal). Thus, weather can directly affect refined product prices; for example, a mild winter would reduce seasonal heating oil demand in the winter season.

Supply is determined by the available refining capacity and the utilization rate of this capacity, which determines the crude run or a refinery's capacity. If it seems that the supply of a certain product (gasoline) is insufficient during a high demand time (the summer driving season), the product's prices will increase. Utilization rates experience a seasonal decline during the refinery maintenance season in the spring (in preparation for gasoline demand in the summer) and in the fall (to prepare for seasonally stronger heating oil production); product prices and refining margins react to lower crude runs owing to reduced capacity utilization rates.

Overall, the global refining industry has been suffering from chronic overcapacity, which has led to reduced capacity utilization over the past few years.

INDUSTRY THEMES

SHALE OIL AND SHALE GAS

Technological advancements have made possible the development of vast supplies in tight oil and gas reservoirs in the US economy in recent years. Tight oil and tight gas are hydrocarbons that are trapped in tight rock formations, which are characterized by very low permeability and low porosity. Hydrocarbons in these tight rock formations cannot flow to the surface without the assistance of technologically advanced drilling methods and completion processes. The application of new technologies made the production of larger volumes from these trapped hydrocarbons possible, thereby making the development of reserves in these tight rock formations economic.

Shale oil and gas is a special type of tight oil and gas formed when the hydrocarbons are trapped in shale rock, with shale acting as the seal to trap the hydrocarbons in the reservoir. Shale rock is a sedimentary rock with ultralow permeability; it typically becomes the reservoir rock in a producing reservoir by sealing the hydrocarbons. In addition, shale sometimes becomes the source rock, transforming into oil and gas hydrocarbons through persistent pressure.

Two techniques have been successfully applied simultaneously to unlock oil and gas locked in these shale formations with ultralow permeability. Horizontal drilling provides greater access to trapped pockets of liquids in tight shale rock formations, and hydraulic fracturing (fracking) cracks open the rock containing the oil and gas by pumping a highly pressurized mix of chemicals and water down into the well. The drilling fluids also contain proppants to keep the cracked source rock open so that the hydrocarbons can continuously flow through the wellbore to the surface.

Hydrocarbons produced from these tight rock formations are known as "unconventional oil and gas" because simple conventional drilling technology (vertical drilling) without hydraulic fracturing and special stimulation methods to support the flow of hydrocarbons would not yield enough production volumes to make the well economic. In contrast, hydrocarbons extracted from sandstone and other reservoir formations with higher porosity and permeability are considered conventional oil and gas. Only the application of unconventional extraction methods will produce enough hydrocarbons to justify the profitable development of shale formations. Thus, the combined application of horizontal drilling and hydraulic fracturing has converted the development of tight and shale reservoirs into a profitable process.

Unconventional shale oil and gas is predominantly found onshore. **Exhibit 26** shows where the largest and most significant shale oil and gas reservoirs are located in the United States.

Exhibit 26. Key Shale Gas and Shale Oil Reservoirs in the United States

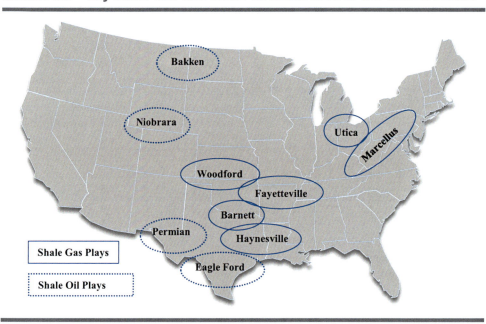

Source: Energy Information Agency.

The future success of unconventional shale oil and gas developments (not just in the United States but also globally) will be highly dependent on the management of environmental risks. Stringent legislation could affect the economics of shale-producing companies, and political resistance might prevent the future drilling licenses from being granted. Water consumption and water contamination from chemicals used in fracking fluids pose serious environmental risks for the industry. Fracking uses 7 million–20 million liters of water per well, of which only about 10%–40% returns to the surface. The use of water-intensive fracking technology becomes very problematic in water-scarce regions, especially if freshwater that would otherwise be available for local drinking water is used in the process. In addition, there have been concerns about the contamination of drinking water; polluted groundwater has been found in isolated incidents.

It is estimated that about 40% of global shale gas reserves are located in regions with limited water supplies. In the United States, Pennsylvania has already suspended water use for fracking purposes in some areas during the drought season. E&P companies are looking to reuse the fracking water that returns to the surface after the initial drilling, but it must be cleaned first because it is contaminated with residual drilling and fracking fluids. In addition, the industry is experimenting with alternative fracking fluids, such as gels or saltwater. As regulation develops in the United States and other countries, costs associated with safely treating and disposing of used fracking water might increase.

US SHALE GAS DEVELOPMENTS

Although the development of shale gas is closely connected to the United States—the first commercial shale gas production was achieved in the Barnett Shale in Texas—the existence of unconventional shale gas reservoirs is not limited to the United States. Such reservoirs can be found around the globe (e.g., China, Argentina, Russia, Australia, West and Central Europe). New production techniques first applied in the United States have made these gas reserves that were previously considered uneconomic very profitable. It is estimated that shale gas represents about one-third of the world's total gas reserves.

It is debatable, however, how quickly and to what degree other shale gas regions can replicate the US success of developing this unconventional gas resource. Global differences in geological shale rock characteristics and the lack of fracturing and horizontal drilling experience, as well as equipment, are often cited as the most important barriers to success outside the United States. In addition, more stringent environmental rules and regulations could slow down shale gas developments in some countries. Finally, land ownership laws outside the United States can also affect the ability of E&P companies to extract hydrocarbons from shale.

Similar to the terminal decline in US oil output, total gas production in the United States started to fall between 2000 and 2005, although the development of new tight gas reservoirs initially helped to offset the steady decline of conventional onshore and offshore gas production. In the mid-2000s, the United States was still expected to become a major LNG importer in order to meet growing domestic gas demand, but the commercial success in the Barnett Shale in 2005 entirely reversed the supply picture with the start of robust production growth from shale formations.

Unconventional drilling in the Barnett Shale started the US shale gas revolution. Subsequently, development commenced in several other reservoirs (Marcellus, Utica Fayetteville, Woodford, and Haynesville). Future production growth is projected to be driven by the vast reserves in the Marcellus shale. Furthermore, the rapid increase in domestically produced shale gas since mid-2000 has persistently kept US natural gas prices low.

Depressed natural gas prices benefit gas-intensive industries (fertilizers and chemicals) by reducing their feedstock costs, whereas energy-intensive manufacturing sectors can operate with lower energy costs. Thus, the US shale gas revolution has triggered a renaissance of the manufacturing industry and supported a switch from coal- to gas-fired electricity generation in the United States. As a result, the industrial and power generation sectors are projected to be the main demand drivers for natural gas going forward.

Growing domestic gas supply from shale gas production has also eliminated the need for US LNG imports. Modest annual demand growth of an estimated 1% on average between 2010 and 2040 will soon be surpassed by an estimated 2% in natural gas supply growth over the same period. Consequently, the United States is currently preparing to become an LNG exporter on a larger scale.

Because domestic natural gas prices are expected to increase in response to LNG exports, the United States will have to find a balance between supporting the gas-producing E&P industry (with higher gas prices) and avoiding damaging the domestic industrial sector (by raising its feedstock and energy costs too much).

As shown in **Exhibit 27**, several LNG export terminals are currently under construction or in the approval process. The US Department of Energy (DOE) has currently approved the export of 12 bcfd (or 90 mtpa) of natural gas as LNG shipments from US terminals.[3] It is highly likely that the allowed LNG export ceiling could be raised if the DOE were to conclude that the impact of LNG exports on domestic US gas prices would only be marginal.

Exhibit 27. Planned US LNG Export Terminals

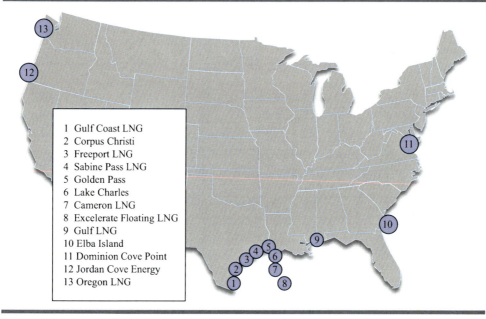

1 Gulf Coast LNG
2 Corpus Christi
3 Freeport LNG
4 Sabine Pass LNG
5 Golden Pass
6 Lake Charles
7 Cameron LNG
8 Excelerate Floating LNG
9 Gulf LNG
10 Elba Island
11 Dominion Cove Point
12 Jordan Cove Energy
13 Oregon LNG

Source: US Energy Information Agency.

---

[3]bcfd = billion cubic feet per day; mtpa = million tons per annum.

LNG exports started in January 2016 with the first cargo of LNG shipped from Cheniere Energy's Sabine Pass LNG plant on the coast of Louisiana. Afterward, LNG exports from the currently constructed Freeport, Cameron, and Corpus Christi terminals on the Gulf Coast and from Cove Point in Maryland should start in 2018–2019. Several other terminals are still in the planning stage (on the US West Coast), which still need regulatory approval from the DOE.

US TIGHT OIL DEVELOPMENTS

After US natural gas prices fell below \$2/mmbtu[4] in April 2012 in response to significant shale gas volumes hitting the US natural gas market, even pure natural gas producers started shifting their drilling programs from dry gas to oil and liquids-rich basins in response to the unprofitable gas price levels that resulted. This switch from gas to oil and liquids-rich-directed drilling was reflected in a significant increase in the US oil rig count between 2010 and 2012. **Appendix 2** covers the underlying rig count data. As a result, tight oil has emerged as a related unconventional theme in the US upstream industry because the same technology (horizontal drilling with multi-stage fracturing) can be applied to vast—and previously considered uneconomic—tight oil reservoirs.

US oil production was in steady decline after peaking just shy of 10 million barrels per day (mbd) in 1970. New volumes from Alaska postponed the terminal decline for 10 years, and in 2007, growing tight oil production stopped the decline at just below 5 mbd and more than offset the natural decline rates of conventional oil in the lower 48 states' onshore and offshore basins. Estimates for future production growth still vary, but a consensus seems to be building that US output could come close to previous peak levels by 2020 (just shy of 10 mbd, according to the US EIA).

Production levels of 9–10 mbd would put the US about in line with Saudi Arabia, possibly enabling it to once again overtake Russia as the largest non-OPEC producer. The projected surge in oil output growth until 2020 will come entirely from new tight oil developments and, in particular, from two shale oil plays—the Bakken in North Dakota and the Eagle Ford in Texas. Conventional production in Texas should hold steady, and offshore developments in the deepwater of the Gulf of Mexico could also add a small growth component. The legacy fields in California and Alaska, however, will probably continue to decline steadily between 2015 and 2025.

The strong revival in US oil output created a global oil surplus in 2014, when global oil supply outstripped weaker oil demand (in particular, from China) and triggered the sudden oil price slump in the second half of 2014. Growing US tight oil supply substituted light crude imports to the United States, which had to be absorbed by other importing countries and increased oil supply in global markets. As a result, WTI and Brent oil prices collapsed by about 50% over six months—to

---

[4]mmbtu = 1 million British thermal units.

$53/bbl and $57/bbl, respectively, by the end of 2014. Prices for both WTI and Brent crude have fallen even further in 2015 and tumbled even below $30/bbl at the beginning of 2016.

An additional reason for the steep oil price decline was OPEC's (or, more accurately, Saudi Arabia's) surprising unwillingness during the OPEC meetings in November 2014 and 2015 to cut production. One reason or OPEC's inaction was that the cartel tried to curb surging US oil output by hurting high-cost tight oil producers in the United States with cheaper oil prices. In addition, Saudi Arabia did not want to lose global market share by unilaterally cutting output to defend prices.

Total economic breakeven costs for tight oil producers vary across different basins and even within the same basin (depending on the oil and gas output mix as well as on transportation costs). Although already-producing wells have fairly low operating costs of $10–$20/bbl for ongoing production, oil prices below $60/bbl could hurt investment in new wells, for which total breakeven costs appear to be on average higher around $50–$60/bbl.

Thus, if oil prices stay below $50/bbl for a prolonged time, the exploration and development of new shale wells in many basins would become uneconomic and could thus be canceled or delayed. Because the initial production of tight oil wells declines very rapidly—by 60%–70% during the first year—any delays in the development of additional wells would also lead to a slowdown in future US production growth. It appears that Saudi Arabia let oil prices slide in the second half of 2014 to test the economic resilience of US tight oil producers to lower oil prices.

Any slowdown in US oil production growth owing to investment cuts in a lower oil price environment, however, is only a temporary phenomenon that cannot permanently derail US tight oil developments. Instead, the industry will eventually adapt to lower oil prices by cutting drilling costs and standardizing fracking techniques in order to further reduce the industry's breakeven costs. Therefore, because US oil output will most likely continue to increase (even if not at the growth rates projected by the EIA), the question remains whether the US could become fully independent from oil imports and even start exporting crude oil (similar to LNG).

Although US crude oil exports are currently not permitted by law under the Jones Act[5] (in contrast, oil products, such as gasoline, have been exported for many years), US political support for exporting some WTI crude oil appears to be growing. Once the US refiners in the Midwest and on the Gulf Coast have absorbed the domestic tight oil production, any incremental volumes coming to the domestic market would weigh on domestic oil prices in the absence of export opportunities. Considering the political sensitivity of national energy security, it is highly uncertain whether and when the US export restriction for crude oil could be even partially or fully lifted.

---

[5]The Jones Act, officially the Merchant Marine Act of 1920, is a US federal legislation that regulates, among other things, maritime commerce.

Even if some exports of US light crude were to be permitted, however, it would not mean that the United States would become a net exporter of crude oil. Total oil demand in the United States (for light and heavier crudes) is dominated by the transportation and industrial sectors and is projected, based on EIA forecasts, to be relatively flat, with small declines until 2040. But even the anticipated near-term increase in total US liquids production (for crude oil, natural gas liquids, ethanol, and biodiesel) would not be sufficient to cover the 18 mbd of total US liquids demand. Although domestic production increases should cause oil and liquids imports to decline in the near term, the United States will remain a net importer of crude oil and liquids for the foreseeable future.

US SHALE GAS AND TIGHT OIL PLAYERS

Small- and medium-sized E&P companies were the pioneers of the shale gas revolution in the United States, which started when Mitchell Energy drilled the first horizontal wells and produced the first shale gas from the Barnett Shale in Texas in 1990 (Devon Energy acquired Mitchell Energy in 2002). These small- and medium-sized players continued to improve horizontal drilling and shale rock fracturing techniques to make the development of shale gas reservoirs economic on a larger scale by mid-2000.

Meanwhile, the big US integrated oil companies, such as ExxonMobil and Chevron, missed the US shale revolution and came late to the party by acquiring already-established shale gas players in order to acquire the technical know-how needed to develop these vast resource basins, which were located in their own backyards. However, many large acquisitions were badly timed because gas prices were still relatively strong when the deals took place. Subsequently, the significant production increase in shale gas volumes started to depress gas prices. For example, ExxonMobil acquired XTO Energy in December 2009 for $31 billion, and Chevron bought much smaller Atlas Energy a year later for $4.3 billion.

The biggest producers in most of the key US shale basins are still small- and medium-cap companies, although the big IOs have gained an initial foothold through their acquisitions. Although ExxonMobil is among the top five shale gas producers in three US shale gas basins, the company is still predominantly an oil producer; the majority of its production comes from oil and liquids produced by its large and diversified portfolio of IO assets.

LIQUEFIED NATURAL GAS

Converting natural gas (methane) into liquefied natural gas (LNG) provides an alternative means of transporting gas from remote locations (so-called stranded gas) to the point of consumption. When the distance to be covered is not too long, natural gas is typically transported via pipelines from the producing fields to its customer base. LNG becomes a viable option, however, when pipeline transportation becomes uneconomic because the gas would have to travel very long distances or pipelines would have to surmount technical difficulties, such as crossing deep oceans.

THE LNG VALUE CHAIN

The LNG value chain consists of several different processes, which are pursued in separate stages and usually by different companies. The produced natural gas is supplied via pipeline to liquefaction plants located on a coastline. The gas is then cooled to –162°C in order to convert it into a liquid state. After the gas has been liquefied and converted into LNG, the LNG is shipped in a liquid state on special-purpose LNG tankers to the consuming markets (primarily Asia). Once the LNG reaches its destination, it is kept in liquid form in onshore storage facilities until it is converted back into a gaseous state (regasified) in special regasification plants. The gas is then transported via pipeline to industrial or power generation customers.

For remote offshore gas reserves, it might become economic to use a floating LNG liquefaction plant (FLNG) instead of transporting the gas via pipeline back to shore to get the gas liquefied in an onshore liquefaction plant. This FLNG technology is still in development, and currently, no FLNGs are in operation. Royal Dutch Shell (RDS) is on track to be the first company to make FLNG technology commercially viable with the anticipated Prelude FLNG plant off the northwest coast of Australia in 2017.

The process of liquefying, shipping, and regasifying LNG along the whole LNG value chain is very capital intensive and requires significant upfront capital investment. Thus, to make an LNG project commercially viable, the produced LNG is sold under long-term (20-year) take-or-pay contracts using predetermined fixed-price formulas to recover the initial capital investment at rather modest rates of return of 10%–15%. Given the long-term nature of LNG contracts, onshore liquefaction plants require the development of large gas reserves (typically more than 5 trillion cubic feet of proved reserves) that provide the feed gas for the LNG project. Because part of the feed gas is also used as an energy fuel during the energy-intensive liquefaction process, about 10%–15% of the feed gas is lost during the conversion process to LNG.

The liquefaction process of converting gas into LNG is the most expensive stage of the LNG value chain; a commercial liquefaction plant costs about $5 billion compared with $1 billion for a regasification plant, which is technologically less challenging. Gas-producing companies tend to invest in liquefaction plants, which are the most capital-intensive parts of the value chain. They also require advanced technological know-how, whereas LNG customers focus their investment on downstream transportation vessels and regasification infrastructure; their primary concern is ensuring the security of the LNG supply to their local markets. Cost inflation owing to rising material and personnel costs has become a pressing issue in the LNG industry and

Industry Themes

has led to cost overruns for the construction of large-scale liquefaction plants, causing project delays and profit warnings by large IO companies.

Exhibit 28 and **Exhibit 29** show the biggest LNG exporting and importing countries as of 2013.

Because the LNG market has been dominated by individual long-term supply contracts between gas-producing LNG exporters (e.g., Qatar) and buyers in Asia (e.g., Japan and South Korea), LNG prices and contract terms are negotiated individually and terms vary by contract. In contrast to spot market pricing in very liquid gas markets in North American (Henry Hub) and the UK (National Balancing Point), gas prices in LNG markets are set by individually negotiated long-term contracts. These LNG contract prices are directly linked to oil prices or an index of different crude oils, such as Japan's Crude Cocktail index, which can be used as a pricing proxy for Asian LNG buyers.

LNG contract prices were initially oil indexed; Japanese buyers used LNG in the 1970s to replace oil with gas as a fuel in power generation. Thus, LNG contract prices still tend to follow oil prices with a six-month time lag. The oil price indexation for long-term LNG contracts has led to significant gas price differentials between depressed US NYMEX (New York Mercantile Exchange) spot prices of $3–$4/mmbtu (because of a significant increase in shale gas production) and higher LNG contract prices of $15–$17/mmbtu in Asia. However, in response to the oil price declines in 2014 and 2015, Asian LNG prices have also tumbled to $8–$9/mmbtu.

In addition to long-term contractual LNG pricing, international oil companies have developed their own LNG trading portfolios by buying LNG under long-term 20-year contracts in order to ship it in their own fleets for direct resale on a short-term or

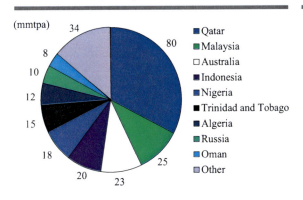

Exhibit 28. LNG Exporters in 2013 (mmtpa)

Sources: IEA and company information.

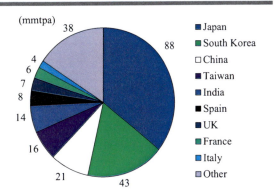

Exhibit 29. LNG Importers in 2013 (mmtpa)

Sources: IEA and company information.

spot basis to dedicated buyers in Asian markets. About one-third of all LNG purchases are estimated to be made by these short-term LNG trades today, in which LNG, which was originally purchased by merchants under long-term contracts, is directly resold into the market to a short-term buyer. BG Group stands out as such an LNG merchant. It has a large shipping fleet and its own regasification capacity.

The start of LNG exports from the United States could disrupt the long-term, oil price–linked LNG contract pricing because US Henry Hub gas prices have always been significantly lower than Asian LNG prices. It is expected that Asian LNG buyers could demand that the formula for long-term LNG contracts will be changed to link LNG prices to lower Henry Hub prices (instead of higher oil prices), not just for US LNG exports but also for long-term supply contracts from the Middle East and Australia.

GLOBAL LNG SUPPLY AND DEMAND

The global LNG market can be split into three supply regions—the Atlantic Basin (including Europe, North and West Africa, and the east coast of North and South America), the Pacific Basin (South Asia, India, Australia, Eastern Russia, and Alaska), and the Middle East Basin (primarily Qatar and, to a lesser extent, the United Arab Emirates and Oman).

Although global LNG supply was dominated by Asian suppliers until 2000 (from Indonesia and Malaysia), Qatar's LNG supply, which comes from the giant North Field (Qatargas 2 and Qatargas 3 in 2009 and 2010, respectively), significantly increased the share of LNG coming from the Middle East region by 2010. In addition, new LNG plants in Egypt and capacity plant expansions in Nigeria and Trinidad and Tobago increased the share of LNG supply from the Atlantic Basin vis-à-vis the Pacific Basin by 2010.

Although Qatar's moratorium on future gas developments will limit incremental Middle East LNG supply, the expected startup of US LNG exports will further increase the share of LNG supply from the Atlantic Basin by 2020. Supply growth in the Pacific Basin will come from several startup plants in Australia. By 2020, LNG supply from the Atlantic Basin and also from the Pacific Basin is expected to surpass Middle East LNG supply, and the Atlantic Basin is expected to become the second-largest supply region after the Pacific Basin.

Demand for LNG has been dominated by buyers from Japan and South Korea. European LNG demand has historically been driven by buyers from Spain and France, and demand from the Americas (primarily the US East Coast) has always accounted for the smallest share. Going forward, the share of LNG demand from Asia Pacific is expected to increase owing to growing demand from India and China. European LNG demand is expected to remain stable until the end of the decade, but demand from the Americas should decline once the United States starts exporting LNG. The global LNG market is expected to remain fairly balanced until the end of

Industry Themes

the decade. After that, the startup of several new LNG plants could alter the global supply–demand balance, result in a slightly oversupplied market.

COMPANY POSITIONING ALONG THE LNG VALUE CHAIN

Large integrated oil producers tend to focus their capital spending on liquefaction assets in order to support the development and monetization of their (stranded) gas reserves in their own liquefaction plants. Given the capital intensity of liquefaction plants, it is primarily large integrated oil companies (i.e., Big Oil) that can afford the large-scale liquefaction projects that would be too expensive for smaller independent E&P companies.

As shown in **Exhibit 30**, RDS and Total own the largest number of liquefaction plants that are currently in operation or under construction. Both also have a relatively high exposure to the downstream regasification business, which is also dominated by several players (CNOOC, Repsol, Petrobras), and little or no ownership of liquefaction plants.

The LNG shipping business is clearly dominated by BG (see **Exhibit 31**), which operates the largest fleet of LNG ships (including ordered ships). BG acts as a trader in the global LNG market by purchasing LNG under long-term contracts and selling flexible volumes to short-term buyers in the spot market, which can be delivered by its own fleet to Asian buyers.

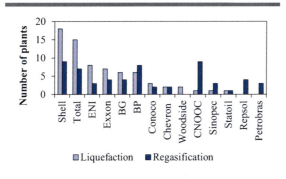

Exhibit 30. LNG Plants (Existing and Planned)

Source: Company information as of 2014.

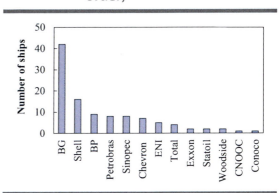

Exhibit 31. LNG Fleet (Operating and On Order)

Source: Company information as of 2014.

FINANCIAL ANALYSIS

OIL AND GAS ACCOUNTING UNDER US GAAP AND IFRS

This guide provides a top-level look at several accounting and reporting issues that are most relevant to the oil and gas sector and summarizes how international accounting standards may differ on these issues. Although the convergence of US GAAP and the International Financial Reporting Standards (IFRS) is an ongoing process between the US Financial Accounting Standards Board (FASB) and the International Accounting Standards Board (IASB), significant differences remain. The conceptual frameworks for US GAAP and IFRS are, in general, very similar, but US GAAP offers more detailed and industry-specific guidance for the oil and gas sector than the IFRS rules.

DIFFERENCES BETWEEN FULL-COST AND SUCCESSFUL EFFORTS ACCOUNTING

The oil and gas sector is the only industry that allows companies to choose from two considerably different financial accounting methods for exploration and production activities according to US GAAP rules: successful efforts or full cost. The methods differ in the way the main cost components in E&P activities are accounted for:

- acquisition costs associated with purchasing or leasing a property or mineral right;

- exploration costs for drilling exploratory and stratigraphic test wells before and after the property has been acquired;

- development costs incurred to obtain access to reserves and related to providing facilities for extracting, treating, gathering, and storing oil and gas;

- production costs for lifting oil and gas to the surface and for gathering, treating, processing, and storing it in the field; and

- treatment of gains and/or losses resulting from the sale of a property or mineral right.

SUCCESSFUL EFFORTS (SE) METHOD

Acquisition and exploration costs are capitalized only under the SE method when minerals are found. All exploration costs related to exploratory dry holes, most geological and geophysical (G&G) costs, and other property-carrying costs are immediately expensed in the year they occur. Development costs, as well as costs that relate to successful exploration wells and to the acquisition of properties for which minerals can later be found, are capitalized. Capitalized costs are then amortized using unit-of-production calculations, in which property acquisition costs are amortized over proved reserves and property development costs over proved developed reserves. Amortization is calculated for capitalized cost pools, which represent single fields (aggregations of individual leases or properties) under the SE method.

FULL-COST (FC) METHOD

Under the FC method, only production costs are immediately expensed through the income statement, and all property acquisition, sale, exploration, and development costs (even dry hole costs) are capitalized as fixed assets.

The costs are then amortized on a country-by-country cost pool basis using a unit-of-production method, which is based on produced oil and gas volumes and the remaining proved reserves. Thus, the countrywide cost pools under the FC method are much larger than the individual field cost pool under the SE method. If the unamortized capitalized costs of oil and gas properties exceed a cost ceiling (the SEC ceiling test) determined by the present value of projected future cash flows from proved reserves, then the excess amount is reported as an impairment loss in the income statement.

To illustrate the difference between SE and FC accounting in a very simple example, assume that a company drills five exploratory wells for $1 million each and hydrocarbons are found in only one of the five wells, which the company would then report as proved reserves. If the company uses SE accounting, it would report a $1 million asset, and the $4 million in exploration costs for four unsuccessful wells would be reported as an exploration expense on the income statement. If the company instead chooses FC accounting, it would report a $5 million asset called "oil and gas property" on the balance sheet, which would be amortized over several years at smaller amounts on the income statement.

The SE method is more conservative than the FC method because income statements of SE companies are forced to report higher expenses with lower operating profits after expensing dry hole costs, G&G costs from unsuccessful drilling efforts, and all general and administrative (G&A) costs. Because FC companies do not report exploration expenses in their accounts, it is already possible to detect a company's respective accounting method on the face of its income statement. **Appendix 3** provides a selection of US companies (E&P and IO) using SE or FC accounting.

These accounting differences make it difficult to directly compare companies using SE and FC accounting; therefore, investors should focus on cash flow–based earnings measures for comparison purposes. As shown in **Exhibit 32**, EBITDAX (earnings before interest, taxes, depreciation, amortization, and exploration) represents a good cash flow proxy that automatically eliminates the most significant differences between SE and FC accounting. In contrast, EBIT (earnings before interest and taxes) and EBITDA (earnings before interest, taxes, depreciation, and amortization) deviate quite noticeably under both methods. If a pure cash flow number is derived after eliminating all capitalization and expensing differences, both methods yield the same cash flow in our example ($26 million).

Exhibit 32. Successful Efforts vs. Full-Cost Accounting

	SE	FC	Comments
Exploration costs (US$ millions)	5.0	5.0	Five wells cost US$1 million each
Reserves (mboe)	5,000	5,000	mboe = thousand barrels of oil equivalent
Production (mboe)	500	500	
Realized price (USD per boe)	70	70	
Revenue (US$ millions)	35.0	35.0	
Production costs (US$ millions)	7.0	7.0	Fully expensed under FC and SE
Exploration expense (US$ millions)	4.0	0.0	No expense under FC; only SE companies expense dry hole costs
General and administrative (G&A) expense (US$ millions)	2.0	1.5	Only FC allows to capitalize the G&A portion of exploration costs
Depreciation, depletion, and amortization (US$ millions)	8.0	8.4	Higher under FC because of higher amortization base from additional capitalized value of exploration expense (9.1% × 4.0 = 0.36)
Depreciation rate	9.1%	9.1%	Unit of production—Amortization: Current production/(Current production + Year-end reserves)
EBIT (US$ millions)	14.0	18.1	
EBITDA (US$ millions)	22.0	26.5	
EBITDAX (US$ millions)	26.0	26.5	
Cash flow *before* exploration expense (US$ millions)	26.0	26.0	Adjusted for US$0.5 million capitalized G&A

Source: Author's calculations.

Under international accounting standards, IFRS 6 (Exploration for and Evaluation of Mineral Resources) governs the accounting for exploration and evaluation (E&E) assets. According to IFRS 6, the company must specify which expenditures are recognized as E&E assets (e.g., expenses for the acquisition of exploration rights, G&G expenses, exploratory drilling, and sampling costs for the technical feasibility and commercial viability of resources), and upon initial recognition, E&E assets should be measured at cost. Development costs should not be recognized as E&E assets.

IFRS 6 allows two accounting policies for E&E assets after initial recognition. Under the cost model, companies should either expense E&E costs as they incur or capitalize E&E costs pending evaluation. Under the revaluation model, E&E assets are classified as intangible or tangible assets and revalued based on IAS (International Accounting Standards) 38 (Intangible Assets) or IAS 16 (Property, Plant and Equipment), respectively. Deferred costs of an undeveloped mineral right may be amortized subject to an impairment test each period, with the amount of impairment charged as expense, or remain deferred until it is determined whether the property holds hydrocarbon reserves.

E&E assets, however, should be reclassified when the technical feasibility and commercial viability of production are demonstrated or when it is determined that no commercial reserves are present. If hydrocarbons are found, the assets should be tested for impairment under IAS 36 (Impairment of Assets) and then reclassified and accounted for under IAS 16 or IAS 38. If no commercial reserves are found, the E&E costs should be expensed.

The application of IFRS 6 is comparable with the FC method during the E&E phase, and it also allows for grouping of cash-generating units (CGUs) when assessing E&E assets for impairment. The SE method and IFRS 6 are very compatible because the basic SE premise (that costs are capitalized pending evaluation) is consistent with IFRS 6. **Exhibit 33** summarizes the main accounting differences among SE, FC, and IFRS.

Exhibit 33. **Comparison of Successful Efforts and Full-Cost Accounting with IFRS Accounting**

	SE (US GAAP)	FC (US GAAP)	IFRS
Unit of account or cost center	Cost center is an individual mineral lease, field, concession, or production-sharing contract	Cost centers are established on a country-by-country basis	No specific guidance for defining a cost center; current industry practice is similar to the SE method
Acquisition costs	Initially capitalized but later expensed if no hydrocarbons can be found	Capitalized	

(continued)

Exhibit 33. Comparison of Successful Efforts and Full-Cost Accounting with IFRS Accounting (continued)

	SE (US GAAP)	FC (US GAAP)	IFRS
Exploration costs	Well costs are initially capitalized at the lease or field level; G&G costs are expensed as incurred	Well costs, G&G costs, and costs for drilling exploratory wells and for dry holes are capitalized	Well costs and G&G costs may be capitalized or expensed, subject to the elected accounting policy
	Costs of drilling exploratory wells are initially capitalized but later charged to expense when no proved reserves can be found; dry holes are expensed as incurred	The costs for dry holes and commercially viable wells are transferred to country-wide full-cost centers and amortized	After well becomes commercial, E&E assets are tested for impairment and reclassified as property, plant and equipment, or intangible assets
	Capitalized costs of commercially viable wells are amortized		The treatment of exploratory wells and dry holes depends on the unit of account and how impairment is assessed
Development costs	Capitalized in cost centers at lease or field levels	Capitalized in cost centers at the country level	No specific accounting standard addresses costs subsequent to the E&E phase; costs should be capitalized if they are expected to provide future economic benefit
Production costs	Expensed as incurred	Expensed as incurred	No specific accounting standard addresses costs subsequent to the E&E phase; costs should be capitalized if they are expected to provide future economic benefit
Impairment	Capitalized costs are subject to impairment provisions	Capitalized costs cannot exceed full-cost center ceiling	E&E costs are grouped in CGUs and tested for impairment
	Unproved properties are assessed periodically for impairment	Unproved properties are excluded from amortization and are at least annually tested for impairment	All assets outside the E&E phase are tested for impairment; impairment loss must be reversed up to the newly estimated recoverable amount (including dry holes)

(continued)

Financial Analysis

Exhibit 33. Comparison of Successful Efforts and Full-Cost Accounting with IFRS Accounting (continued)

	SE (US GAAP)	FC (US GAAP)	IFRS
Depreciation, depletion, and amortization (DD&A)	DD&A is calculated on a unit-of-production basis for individual cost centers at the lease or field level	DD&A is calculated on a unit-of-production basis for individual cost centers at the countrywide level	DD&A can be calculated with a variety of depreciation methods (including the unit-of-production basis); no guidance is given for the selection of the cost center or unit of account
	Proved property acquisition costs are depreciated over total proved reserves; costs for wells and equipment are depreciated over proved developed reserves	Capitalized costs for acquisition, exploration, and development are depreciated over total proved reserves	Not defined over which reserve base capitalized costs should be depreciated, but proper matching of costs and production requires that, no matter which reserve base is chosen, all costs applicable to that reserve category are included in the amortization base

INVENTORY ACCOUNTING

Crude oil, products, and merchandise inventories are valued at the lower end of current market value or cost under both US GAAP and IFRS. US GAAP, however, allows companies to use the LIFO (last-in, first-out) method to determine the cost of crude oil inventories, whereas IFRS prohibits LIFO valuation. Therefore, IFRS-compliant oil and gas companies have to use the FIFO (first-in, first-out) inventory valuation to calculate the value of their oil and product inventories.

Refining and chemical companies hold significant volumes of oil inventories because crude oil is the main feedstock in their oil product or chemicals production. FIFO inventory valuation requires IFRS-compliant companies to use the oldest inventory purchases (or even those from previous periods) as the relevant costs for matching product sales in the current period, which can severely distort company profits during times of volatile oil prices. Under FIFO accounting, profits could be understated during times of significant oil price declines or would be overstated when oil prices quickly increase over the course of a reporting period.

Therefore, refining companies or IO companies with downstream operations often provide alternative earnings calculations in addition to their IFRS-compliant reported profits in an effort to eliminate the distorting FIFO effect. These additional "clean"

EBITDA or "clean" earnings measures are an attempt to provide an approximation of how the company's underlying operating or net profit would have looked if the most recent crude oil feedstock purchases in that reporting period had been applied as the cost of sales in that same period (thereby assuming a pro forma LIFO inventory valuation).

Alternatively, Royal Dutch Shell (RDS) uses an industry measure called "current cost of supply" (CCS) to value the cost of its oil feedstock in its downstream (refining and chemicals) division in its quarterly financial statements. The applied CCS method is neither FIFO nor LIFO compliant and, therefore, is not recognized under US GAAP or IFRS. Instead, RDS applies a weighted cost pricing methodology under which the cost of goods sold (oil products and chemicals) during the period is based on the estimated current cost of supplies during the same period. Thus, CCS accounting excludes the effect of changes in the oil price on feedstock inventory costs and better matches the average costs and revenues of sold products during the same reporting period. However, because CCS accounting is not IFRS (or US GAAP) compliant, RDS can only show the calculated CCS earnings in addition to the reported IFRS earnings number in its quarterly results.

OIL AND GAS RESERVES DISCLOSURES

Oil- and gas-producing companies that are listed in the United States have to provide specific reserve-related information under US GAAP. Financial Accounting Standard (FAS) 69, "Disclosures about Oil and Gas Producing Activities," requires that every publicly traded enterprise with significant oil and gas activities (at least 10% of the company's total activities) must disclose the following supplemental information regarding reserves with its annual financial statements:

- Proved oil and gas reserves quantities as a non-value-based disclosure
- A standardized measure of discounted future net cash flows relating to proved oil and gas reserves quantities as a value-based disclosure

Although IFRS do not require specific reserves disclosures, oil and gas companies still need to address reserves and related information under IFRS to provide investors with the information they need to understand the company's financial position and financial performance. Because certain national stock exchanges do require reserves disclosures, companies that prepare their financial statements under IFRS typically follow their national regulatory standards for reserves disclosures. For example, the United Kingdom permits disclosure of either proved or probable developed and undeveloped reserves. The SEC requires that foreign IFRS-reporting oil and gas companies provide their reserves disclosures according to FAS 69.

NON-VALUE RESERVE DISCLOSURES

FAS 69 requires publicly traded companies to disclose information about the quantities of their proved oil and gas reserves annually as supplemental information in their financial statements.

RESERVE QUANTITIES

Companies must report the net quantities of proved developed and undeveloped reserves of crude oil (including condensate and natural gas liquids) and natural gas at the beginning and end of each financial year. If the entity issues consolidated financial statements, reserve disclosures include 100% of the reserves attributable to the parent company and 100% of the reserves attributable to its consolidated subsidiaries.

Reserves of proportionally consolidated subsidiaries should include only the proportionate share of the subsidiary's oil and gas reserves. Reserves of subsidiaries accounted for by the equity method should not be included in the group's oil and gas reserves. Instead, the oil and gas reserves of these "at equity" accounted subsidiaries must be reported separately.

CHANGES IN RESERVE QUANTITIES

Companies must report the changes in net quantities of proved oil and gas reserves during the course of the financial year. The following reasons for reserve changes must be shown separately.

1. Revisions of previous estimates. These revisions reflect upward or downward changes in previous reserve estimates owing to new information obtained from development drilling, production history, or a change in economic factors.

2. Improved recovery. A significant increase in reserve estimates owing to the application of improved recovery techniques must be shown separately, whereas insignificant additions can be included in revisions of previous estimates.

3. Purchase of minerals in place. An increase in the reserve base from the purchase of new acreage containing proved reserves must be shown separately.

4. Extensions and discoveries. This category includes extensions of the proved acreage of previously discovered reserves through additional drilling subsequent to discovery and the discovery of new fields with proved reserves.

5. Production. The reduction in proved reserves resulting from depleting the resource base by producing oil and gas volumes during the financial year must be shown separately.

6. Sales of minerals in place. A decline in the reserve base because of the sale of acreage containing proved reserves must be shown separately.

FAS 69 requires that reserve quantities and changes in reserve quantities be disclosed separately for the company's home country and each foreign geographic area (individual countries or groups of countries) where significant reserves are located.

Exhibit 34 summarizes the oil and gas reserve information provided by Apache in its 2014 annual report.

Exhibit 34. Apache Corp: Oil and Gas Reserve Information

	Crude Oil and Condensate (thousands of barrels)						
	United States	Canada	Egypt	Australia	North Sea	Argentina	Total
Proved developed reserves							
31 December 2012	474,837	79,695	106,746	29,053	119,635	15,845	825,811
31 December 2013	457,981	80,526	119,242	22,524	100,327	14,195	794,795
31 December 2014	444,440	75,876	128,712	29,996	105,746	—	784,770
Proved undeveloped reserves							
31 December 2012	203,068	70,650	17,288	34,808	28,019	2,981	356,814
31 December 2013	195,835	56,366	16,302	36,703	29,253	2,231	336,690
31 December 2014	170,125	59,923	14,617	25,775	19,059	—	289,499
Total proved reserves							
Balance 31 December 2012	677,905	150,345	124,034	63,861	147,654	18,826	1,182,625
Extensions, discoveries, and other additions	133,227	10,177	43,738	2,539	1,543	998	192,222
Purchase of minerals in place	85	—	5	—	3,623	—	3,713
Revisions of previous estimates	1,683	−531	457	−118	18	24	1,533
Production	−53,621	−6,469	−32,690	−7,055	−23,258	−3,422	−126,515
Sale of properties	−105,463	−16,630	—	—	—	—	−122,093

(continued)

Exhibit 34. Apache Corp: Oil and Gas Reserve Information (continued)

	Crude Oil and Condensate (thousands of barrels)						
	United States	Canada	Egypt	Australia	North Sea	Argentina	Total
Balance 31 December 2013	653,816	136,892	135,544	59,227	129,580	16,426	1,131,485
Extensions, discoveries, and other additions	57,011	9,657	38,074	4,254	17,386	5	126,387
Purchase of minerals in place	15,240	—	—	—	—	—	15,240
Revisions of previous estimates	3,083	−812	1,801	−216	−7	—	3,849
Production	−48,789	−6,421	−32,090	−7,494	−22,154	−620	−117,568
Sale of properties	−65,796	−3,517	—	—	—	−15,811	−85,124
Balance 31 December 2014	614,565	135,799	143,329	55,771	124,805	—	1,074,269

	Natural Gas Liquids (thousands of barrels)						
	United States	Canada	Egypt	Australia	North Sea	Argentina	Total
Proved developed reserves							
31 December 2012	154,508	21,996	—	—	2,438	5,007	183,949
31 December 2013	184,485	26,099	—	—	2,435	4,110	217,129
31 December 2014	183,565	17,947	1,346	—	1,770	—	204,628
Proved undeveloped reserves							
31 December 2012	60,889	12,258	—	—	380	876	74,403
31 December 2013	63,538	9,970	—	—	215	1,009	74,732
31 December 2014	69,828	7,168	212	—	371	—	77,579
Total proved reserves							
Balance 31 December 2012	215,397	34,254	—	—	2,818	5,883	258,352
Extensions, discoveries, and other additions	69,231	4,014	—	—	—	—	73,245

(continued)

Exhibit 34. Apache Corp: Oil and Gas Reserve Information (continued)

	Natural Gas Liquids (thousands of barrels)						
	United States	Canada	Egypt	Australia	North Sea	Argentina	Total
Purchase of minerals in place	45	—	—	—	295	—	340
Revisions of previous estimates	1,591	546	—	—	1	3	2,141
Production	–19,922	–2,442	—	—	–464	–767	–23,595
Sale of properties	–18,319	–303	—	—	—	—	–18,622
Balance 31 December 2013	248,023	36,069	—	—	2,650	5,119	291,861
Extensions, discoveries, and other additions	47,516	1,163	1,820	—	1	—	50,500
Purchase of minerals in place	2,916	—	—	—	—	—	2,916
Revisions of previous estimates	2,594	116	–17	—	–2	—	2,691
Production	–21,464	–2,256	–245	—	–508	–116	–24,589
Sale of properties	–26,192	–9,977	—	—	—	–5,003	–41,172
Balance 31 December 2014	253,393	25,115	1,558	—	2,141	—	282,207

	Natural Gas (millions of cubic feet)						
	United States	Canada	Egypt	Australia	North Sea	Argentina	Total
Proved developed reserves							
31 December 2012	2,353,587	1,734,657	690,436	596,052	93,319	365,054	5,833,105
31 December 2013	2,005,966	1,294,420	621,825	626,543	88,177	289,133	4,926,064
31 December 2014	1,616,504	990,145	637,187	640,265	87,259	—	3,971,360
Proved undeveloped reserves							
31 December 2012	832,320	403,227	205,055	1,074,018	18,985	97,496	2,631,101
31 December 2013	667,160	439,037	190,355	975,224	18,988	121,584	2,412,348
31 December 2014	580,299	527,623	171,696	964,554	23,228	—	2,267,400

(continued)

Exhibit 34. Apache Corp: Oil and Gas Reserve Information (continued)

	Natural Gas (millions of cubic feet)						
	United States	Canada	Egypt	Australia	North Sea	Argentina	Total
Total proved reserves							
Balance 31 December 2012	3,185,907	2,137,884	895,491	1,670,070	112,304	462,550	8,464,206
Extensions, discoveries, and other additions	306,721	359,493	44,382	13,351	2,750	16,515	743,212
Purchase of minerals in place	855	—	—	—	10,680	—	11,535
Revisions of previous estimates	61,247	109,551	2,413	–101	32	49	173,191
Production	–285,187	–181,593	130,106	–81,553	–18,601	–68,397	–765,437
Sale of properties	–596,417	–691,878	—	—	—	—	1,288,295
Balance 31 December 2013	2,673,126	1,733,457	812,180	1,601,767	107,165	410,717	7,338,412
Extensions, discoveries, and other additions	203,318	383,077	125,899	81,156	23,803	—	817,253
Purchase of minerals in place	21,337	—	—	—	—	—	21,337
Revisions of previous estimates	35,910	–12,626	5949	—	–54	—	29,179
Production	–215,829	–117,816	135,145	–78,104	–20,427	–12,722	–580,043
Sale of properties	–521,059	–468,324	—	—	—	–397,995	1,387,378
Balance 31 December 2014	2,196,803	1,517,768	808,883	1,604,819	110,487	—	6,238,760

	Total Reserves (thousand barrels of oil equivalent)						
	United States	Canada	Egypt	Australia	North Sea	Argentina	Total
Proved developed reserves							
31 December 2012	1,021,610	390,800	221,819	128,395	137,626	81,695	1,981,945
31 December 2013	976,795	322,362	222,880	126,948	117,457	66,494	1,832,936
31 December 2014	897,422	258,848	236,256	136,707	122,058	—	1,651,291

(continued)

Exhibit 34. Apache Corp: Oil and Gas Reserve Information (continued)

	Total Reserves (thousand barrels of oil equivalent)						
	United States	Canada	Egypt	Australia	North Sea	Argentina	Total
Proved undeveloped reserves							
31 December 2012	402,677	150,113	51,464	213,811	31,563	20,106	869,734
31 December 2013	370,566	139,509	48,028	199,240	32,633	23,504	813,480
31 December 2014	336,670	155,028	43,446	186,534	23,301	—	744,979
Total proved reserves							
Balance 31 December 2012	1,424,287	540,913	273,283	342,206	169,189	101,801	2,851,679
Extensions, discoveries, and other additions	253,578	74,107	51,135	4,764	2,001	3,751	389,336
Purchase of minerals in place	273	—	5	—	5,698	—	5,976
Revisions of previous estimates	13,482	18,274	859	–135	24	35	32,539
Production	–121,074	–39,177	–54,374	–20,647	–26,822	–15,589	–277,683
Sale of properties	–223,185	132,246	—	—	—	—	–355,431
Balance 31 December 2013	1,347,361	461,871	270,908	326,188	150,090	89,998	2,646,416
Extensions, discoveries, and other additions	138,413	74,666	60,877	17,780	21,354	5	313,095
Purchase of minerals in place	21,712	—	—	—	—	—	21,712
Revisions of previous estimates	11,662	–2,800	2,776	–216	–18	—	11,404
Production	–106,225	–28,313	–54,859	–20,511	–26,067	2,856	–238,831
Sale of properties	–178,831	–91,548	—	—	—	–87,147	–357,526
Balance 31 December 2014	1,234,092	413,876	279,702	323,241	145,359	—	2,396,270

Note: Natural gas reserves are converted into units of oil equivalents (boe) by applying a ratio per barrel of oil: Millions of cubic feet/6 = Thousands boe.
Source: Apache Corporation, "2014 Annual Report" (10-K filing with the SEC).

VALUE-BASED RESERVE DISCLOSURES

In addition to requiring information about the reserve *quantities*, FAS 69 requires the calculation of an estimated *value* for the reported oil and gas reserves. FAS 69 requires the disclosure of a "standardized measure of discounted future net cash flows relating to proved oil and gas reserve quantities" at the end of each year, which is commonly abbreviated as the SMOG (standardized measure of oil and gas). Proved reserves reflect the P1 or P90 reserve category (see the Oil and Gas Reserves section), which are recoverable with little risk and a high degree of certainty (i.e., 90% probability).

Based on a typical discounted cash flow (DCF) calculation, the SMOG suffers from the same shortcomings as any forward-looking DCF model—namely, underlying assumptions about future volumes and costs as well as the chosen discount rate. In addition, the SMOG applies a backward-looking component (year-end oil and gas prices) to calculate forward-looking cash flows. Therefore, SMOG appears to be an appropriate acronym for this value-based reserve disclosure; it should not be mistaken as a crystal-clear fair-value measure for the company or its reserves but rather as a hazy reflection of the company's reserve value.

FAS 69 requires the company to disclose the following information for the SMOG calculation of its total proved reserves in each of the geographic regions for which the reserve quantities were previously disclosed.

1. Future cash inflows. Cash flows are calculated using the average oil and gas prices during the 12-month period prior to the ending date of the balance sheet, determined as the unweighted arithmetic average of the oil and gas prices on the first day of the month for each of the previous 12 months. These historical 12-month average oil and gas prices are applied to the year-end oil and gas quantities of the company's proved reserves. Future prices may only be considered if contractual agreements (hedging of future oil and gas prices) are in place at the end of the year.

2. Future development and production costs. These costs reflect the estimated expenditures that are required to develop and produce the proved oil and gas reserves at the end of the year. These expenditures must be calculated based on year-end costs and assume the continuation of existing economic conditions.

3. Future income tax expenses. These expenses are calculated by applying the year-end statutory tax rate to the projected future net cash flows generated from the company's proved oil and gas reserves. These future tax expenses have to consider tax credits and allowances related to the company's proved oil and gas reserves.

4. Future net cash flows. These are calculated as the difference between (1) future cash inflows and (2) future development and production costs as well as (3) future income tax expenses: (1) less (2) less (3).

5. Discount. FAS 69 requires that a 10% discount rate be applied to discount the (4) future net cash flows.

6. Standardized measure of discounted future net cash flows. The difference between (4) future net cash flows and (5) the computed discount: (4) less (5).

Exhibit 35 shows Apache's SMOG calculation based on the required FAS 69 disclosures and relating to the year-end oil and gas reserve quantities shown in the

Exhibit 35. Apache Corp: SMOG for 2013 and 2014
(US$ millions)

	United States	Canada	Egypt	Australia	North Sea	Argentina	Total
2013							
Cash inflows	79,654	19,260	16,864	20,637	15,359	2,824	154,598
Future production costs	−26,032	−8,105	−2,590	−4,494	−8,147	−1,176	−50,544
Future development costs	−4,834	−2,458	−1,899	−2,283	−3,284	−397	−15,155
Future income tax expenses	−12,832	−678	−4,328	−3,072	−2,376	−142	−23,428
Future net cash flows	35,956	8,019	8,047	10,788	1,552	1,109	65,471
10% discount rate	−20,117	−3,987	−2,193	−6,423	85	−242	−32,877
Discounted future net cash flows	15,839	4,032	5,854	4,365	1,637	867	32,594
2014							
Cash inflows	73,859	18,966	16,802	19,391	13,916	—	142,934
Future production costs	−25,875	−7,537	−2,924	−4,105	−7,121	—	−47,562
Future development costs	−4,422	−2,453	−1,683	−1,173	−2,776	—	−12,507
Future income tax expenses	−10,657	−1,070	−4,091	−3,202	−2,445	—	−21,465
Future net cash flows	32,905	7,906	8,104	10,911	1,574	—	61,400
10% discount rate	−17,639	−3,983	−2,099	−5,875	−146	—	−29,742
Discounted future net cash flows	15,266	3,923	6,005	5,036	1,428	—	31,658

Source: Apache Corporation, "2014 Annual Report" (10-K filing with the SEC).

previous section. As required by FAS 69, the SMOG calculation is disclosed for the same countries that were used to categorize the oil and gas reserves.

The SMOG calculation derives a net present value of $31.658 billion for Apache's proved oil and gas reserves at the end of 2014, or $84 per share based on 377 million shares outstanding. In order to convert this reserve-based asset value into an equity value for the company, Apache's net debt ($10.5 billion, or $27.8/share) and minority interests ($2.2 billion, or $5.8/share) at the end of 2014 need to be deducted from the SMOG value, which leaves a SMOG-derived equity value of $50 for Apache at the end of 2014.

Compared with Apache's share price range of $40–$70 in 2015, it could be argued that for most of 2015, the stock has been trading at a premium to its SMOG-derived net present value of its proved reserves. But again, the SMOG value of oil and gas reserves, which is provided by the company, is not commonly used as a relevant valuation metric or as an estimate of the intrinsic value for a specific E&P company.

Because the SMOG calculation uses historical oil and gas prices and considers only future oil and gas production from proved reserves, SMOG values are considered too pessimistic; they do not take any future prospects from the development of probable or even possible reserves into consideration. As a result, the SMOG value tends to be lower than the share price, which usually also reflects the possible future upside potential by discounting the possible success of new developments or discoveries. In the case of Apache, because its share price has been trading mostly above its more conservative SMOG-derived equity value of $50, the share price premium seems to reflect market expectations about the future upside potential from probable reserves.

In addition to the year-end present values for oil and gas reserves based on the SMOG calculation, FAS 69 requires that companies disclose the aggregate change in the SMOG value and the reasons for the change in the reserve value. The value of Apache's proved oil and gas reserves declined by $936 million—from $32.594 billion at the end of 2013 to $31.658 billion at the end of 2014. **Exhibit 36** summarizes the reasons for this decline based on the categories.

Exhibit 36. Apache Corp: Change in SMOG Value from 2013 to 2014
(US$ millions)

Discounted future net cash flows in 2013	32,594
Change in sales, net of production costs	–10,350
Net change in prices and production costs	–1,029
Net change because of extensions, discoveries, and improved recovery	6,297
Changes in estimated future development costs	–1,136
Previously estimated development costs incurred during the period	4,462
Net change because of revisions in quantity estimates	256
Net change because of purchases and sales of minerals in place	508
Accretion of discount	4,442
Change in income taxes	836
Sale of properties	–4,780
Change in production rates and other	–442
Total change in discounted future net cash flows	–936
Discounted future net cash flows in 2014	31,658

Source: Apache Corporation, "2014 Annual Report" (10-K filing with the SEC).

FINANCIAL STATEMENT ANALYSIS

For the purpose of analyzing financial statements (and, in the next section, valuation multiples), I have created a hypothetical company for each of the six analyzed energy subsectors by aggregating the historical financial data of the constituent companies in each of these subsectors: exploration and production, integrated oils, refining and marketing, oil field services, engineering and construction, and contract drilling industries. For example, by adding up the balance sheets and income statements of the largest 15 IO companies in US dollars in each year from 2000 to 2014, I derived the aggregated annual financial information for Integrated Oils Inc. for the past 15 years. The aggregated balance sheets and income statements are used to reflect the financial information for the entire IO subsector in this report.

In a similar fashion, I used the aggregated financial information for each of the six analyzed energy subsectors to compare the balance sheet structure, income statement, and profitability and margins trends among the different subindustries. Within the E&P subsector, the three E&P categories are further classified into international E&P companies and US E&P companies that use FC accounting and US E&P companies that use SE accounting. Therefore, this subsector includes 35 constituent companies, whereas all other subsectors contain only the 10–15 largest companies in their industry.

Appendix 4 provides a full list of all the constituent companies in each subsector. The balance sheets and income statements of these companies are aggregated to derive consolidated financials for each energy subsector. I use the same companies to create separate subsector indexes for the analysis of relative share price performances and to compare valuation multiples among these subsectors. The historical fundamental data for the financial statement analysis, as well as for the pricing information and valuation multiples used in this report, were provided by FactSet's Fundamentals Database.

BALANCE SHEET STRUCTURE

Exhibit 37 summarizes the key balance sheet items for each of the subsectors, expressed as a percentage of total assets. The balance sheet items for all companies included in each subsector universe are summed up annually between 2000 and 2014 to derive an aggregated subsector balance sheet. Each balance sheet item (e.g., a subsector's total current assets) is then calculated as a percentage of the subsector's balance sheet total (or total assets). In addition, **Appendix 5** summarizes some key balance sheet ratios for each energy subsector for the years between 2000 and 2014.

Exhibit 37 shows the average value of the annual percentages between 2000 and 2014 in each subsector. For example, between 2000 and 2014, net property, plant, and equipment (net PP&E) accounted for 79%, on average, of the total assets in US E&P companies under FC accounting, whereas net PP&E made up only 25%, on average, of total assets for oil field services companies during the 15-year time frame. As the percentage values for each balance sheet item were fairly stable (±5%–10%) during the 15-year period, it is reasonable to express them as average values in order to highlight differences in the balance sheet structure among different oil and gas subsectors.

One of the noticeable differences in the balance sheet structure is asset intensity, which is measured as a balance sheet ratio and expressed as the share of net PP&E relative to total assets. It comes as no surprise that US E&P companies using FC accounting have the highest asset intensity (79%) because they can capitalize all of their exploration costs and report them as assets (oil and gas properties), whereas US E&P companies using SE accounting have to expense most of their exploration costs directly through the income statement, with the exception of costs related to successful exploration wells (see the previous section for more detail on SE versus FC accounting).

This accounting difference for exploration costs explains the significantly higher asset intensity for US E&P companies using FC accounting than for US E&P companies using SE accounting, whereas international E&P companies also tend to have a

Exhibit 37. Balance Sheet Structure of Analyzed Energy Subsectors

Balance sheet structure (percentage of total assets, averages for 2000–2014)	Exploration and Production			Integrated Oils	Refining and Marketing	Oil Field Services	Engineering and Construction	Contract Drilling
	US SE	US FC	International					
Cash and short-term investments	3%	4%	12%	5%	12%	10%	13%	10%
Other current assets	13	7	22	19	28	34	36	11
Total current assets	17%	11%	34%	24%	40%	44%	48%	21%
Net property, plant, and equipment	66	79	56	63	38	25	32	68
Other long-term assets	17	10	11	13	22	31	19	11
Long-term assets	83	89	66	76	60	56	52	79
Total assets	100	100	100	100	100	100	100	100
Current liabilities (without debt)	15	9	20	13	22	20	35	8
Long-term liabilities (without debt)	20	17	15	7	8	7	4	7
Total interest-bearing debt	20	27	10	17	35	22	19	31
Total equity	45	47	55	62	35	51	42	54
Total liabilities and shareholders' equity	100%	100%	100%	100%	100%	100%	100%	100%
Net debt/equity	38%	51%	−2%	19%	73%	26%	16%	41%
Current ratio	1.2×	1.2×	1.7×	1.8×	1.9×	2.2×	1.4×	2.6×

Notes: US SE are US E&P companies using successful efforts accounting; US FC are US E&P companies using full-cost accounting; and International are international (non-US) E&P companies. See Appendix 4 for a list of the companies included in each energy subsector.
Source: FactSet.

lower asset intensity because they use an IFRS version of SE accounting. In general, the asset intensity for E&P companies and IOs is higher than for the group of services companies, with the exception of contract drilling companies (which operate a fleet of expensive and capital-intensive drilling rigs).

At the lower end of the asset intensity spectrum are oil field services companies, which provide less capital-intensive drilling and completion services, and E&C companies, which tend to outsource the capital-intensive parts of their construction projects to third-party subcontractors. Although E&C companies can keep their capital intensity at relatively low levels (compared with their E&P and IO peers), they face the risk of project cost overruns when the procurement costs for the outsourced parts from suppliers unexpectedly increase.

The project work of E&C companies is based on long-term contracts, which leads to timing differences between cash paid and received for (sub-) contract work that was received and rendered. These matching or accrual differences lead to higher levels of receivables, payables, and received prepayments on the balance sheets of E&C companies, which explains why E&C companies have the highest shares of average cash (13%) and current assets and liabilities (48% and 35%, respectively).

Net gearing (net debt or cash as a percentage of shareholders' equity) also varies significantly between the analyzed energy subsectors. Although US E&P companies reported net debt levels of 38% (SE) and 51% (FC), on average, at the consolidated subsector level between 2000 and 2014, their international E&P peers have benefited from an average net cash position of 2% during this time frame. In fact, the group of companies included in our international E&P subsector has consistently reported net cash positions at the consolidated subsector level between 2004 and 2012, which seems to reflect a much more conservative financing policy compared with their more debt-financed US E&P peers.

On average, refining and contract drilling companies reported rather high net gearing (i.e., financial leverage) levels, of 73% and 41%, respectively, for the time period between 2000 and 2014. The trends of these net gearing levels, however, have been moving in opposite directions. Debt levels in the refining subsector have declined from extremely high levels (above 100% in 2000–2002) to 50%–60% in recent years, but net gearing in the drilling subsector has increased from 30% in 2000 to 50% by 2014.

The balance sheet structure of IO companies confirms their defensive financial position based on the highest equity share (on average, 62% of total assets) and the second-lowest share of interest-bearing debt (17%) among all energy subsectors. This favorable combination results in a low average net gearing of just 19% at the consolidated subsector level for the past 15 years. The net gearing has also been fairly stable at levels between 15% and 25% annually from 2000 until 2014.

INCOME STATEMENT AND PROFITABILITY

Exhibit 38 shows the profitability ratios and return indicators relating to income statement items for each of the analyzed subsectors. I summed the annual income statements of all companies, which are included in each respective subsector, to derive aggregated subsector income statements for all years from 2000 to 2014. The profitability ratios and return indicators were calculated at the aggregated subsector level, and Exhibit 38 summarizes the 15-year averages of these aggregated values between 2000 and 2014.

Because these numbers represent only 15-year averages, it is also important to analyze their underlying trend and cyclicality between 2000 and 2014 (more so than for the previously shown averages relating to the balance sheet structure, which were fairly stable over the analyzed time frame). Therefore, **Appendix 6** provides these profitability ratios and return indicators on an annual basis between 2000 and 2014.

Although all subsectors have reached double-digit sales growth at comparable levels, on average, profit margins and return on equity or capital employed reveal significant differences among several subindustries. E&P and contract drilling companies, on average, achieve the highest profit margins, whereas the refining sector sits at the lower end of the profit margin spectrum.

Exhibit 38. Profitability and Return Comparisons between Energy Subsectors

Profit Margins and Returns (averages for 2000–2014)	Exploration and Production	Integrated Oils	Refining and Marketing	Oil Field Services	Engineering and Construction	Contract Drilling
Sales growth	17%	15%	20%	11%	17%	17%
EBITDA margin	31	18	7	20	15	38
EBIT margin	20	13	5	14	10	25
Net margin	13	8	3	9	6	17
Capex (% of sales)	26	12	5	10	9	31
Dividend payout ratio[a]	23%	25%	19%	23%	38%	26%
EBIT interest coverage	10.1×	17.1×	4.4×	15.4×	8.8×	7.7×
ROE[b]	18%	19%	16%	16%	14%	13%
ROCE[b]	21%	25%	14%	18%	19%	13%

Note: See Appendix 4 for a list of the companies included in each energy subsector.
[a]Dividend payout ratio is calculated as cash dividends paid relative to net profit reported during the respective calendar year.
[b]ROE and ROCE are calculated on average shareholders' equity and average capital employed during each year.
Source: FactSet.

Revenues and profit margins for oil- and gas-producing E&P and IO companies are primarily driven by rising oil prices; high oil price levels tend to depress profit margins for refining companies.

As oil prices increase, the feedstock costs for refineries rise as well, but refiners may not be able to fully pass these cost increases on by raising prices for their refined products (e.g., gasoline and heating oil). IO companies have lower profit margins than pure E&P companies because they are essentially E&P companies with low-margin refining operations.

Oil prices only indirectly affect revenues and profit margins of the oil services segment (oil field services, E&C, and contract drillers) because their revenue and profit source is the capital spending and drilling activity of their customers (E&P and IO companies), which directly depend on actual oil price levels as much as on future oil price expectations. The (oil price–dependent) activity level for exploration and development drilling by E&P and IO companies directly affects the relevant prices in each of the services segments: pressure-pumping prices for oil field services providers, prices for large construction projects in the E&C sector, and rig rates for contract drilling companies.

Because the exploration and development drilling activity of E&Ps and IOs follows oil prices with a time lag, the prices of oil services (e.g., pressure pumping) also tend to trail oil price development. Prices for oil services are affected by capacity (supply) developments in each of the services industries in addition to oil services demand coming from E&P and IO companies' customers.

The annual sales growth and EBITDA margin changes at the subsector level seem to confirm these trends. Sales growth in oil-producing subsectors (E&P and IO companies) and in the oil-servicing segments (OS and E&C companies) follows the same industry cycle, as shown in **Exhibit 39**, because both groups hit their cyclical troughs in 2002 and in 2009 (with the next trough probably coming in 2015). Sales in the OS and E&C services sectors, however, tend to peak with a one-year time lag compared with their E&P and IO customers. Sales growth for E&C companies appears to be less cyclical because revenue recognition under percentage of completion accounting helps them to smooth the revenue collection process for long-term contracts.

Profitability based on EBITDA margins is highest in the E&P, drilling, and OS subsectors, but operating margins in these subsectors are also more volatile compared with IO companies and the refining industry (see **Exhibit 40**). Similar to sales growth, the profit cycle in the services industries (OS and CD) trails that of their oil-producing clients; EBITDA margins for E&P and IO companies tend to reach their peaks and find their troughs a few years earlier than those for the OS and CD subsectors.

It should be noted that EBITDA margins of the IO subsector have been the least volatile; they have only fluctuated between 16% and 21% from 2000 until 2006.

Exhibit 39. Sales Growth

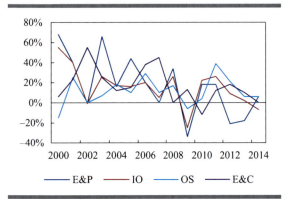

Note: E&P is exploration and production, IO is integrated oils, OS is oil field services, E&C is engineering and construction, R&M is refining and marketing, and CD is contract drilling.
Source: FactSet.

Exhibit 40. EBITDA Margin

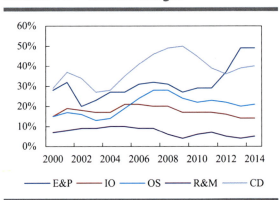

Note: E&P is exploration and production, IO is integrated oils, OS is oil field services, E&C is engineering and construction, R&M is refining and marketing, and CD is contract drilling.
Source: FactSet.

But after EBITDA margins peaked at 21% in 2006, the aggregated margins of the IO subsector have continuously declined to 14% in 2014.

A review of the return on capital employed (ROCE) ratio confirms the trend I described of the tendency of profits in the oil-producing E&P and IO subsectors to peak before those of their oil services peers (OS and CD), which reach their highs a few years later, as shown in **Exhibit 41**. ROCE for the oil-producing E&P and IO subsectors peaked in 2005–2006 before returns for the oil services segments (OS and CD) reached their peaks in 2006–2007.

It is worth pointing out to investors that the relative ranking between the IO and CD subsectors changed when comparing their relative profitability (EBITDA margin) and ROCE levels. Although drillers posted the highest profitability—with an average EBITDA margin of 38% between 2000 and 2014—margins of the IO subsector remained at the lower end of the subsector range. Conversely, the CD subsector dropped to the bottom of the range in terms of ROCE (average of 13% in 2000–2014), whereas IOs moved to the top of the subsector table with an average ROCE of 25%.

This divergence between margins and returns can be explained by each subsector's level of capital intensity (expressed as annual capex as a percentage of sales). Drillers have had the highest average capital intensity over the past 15 years (before E&P companies)—see Exhibit 38 and **Exhibit 42**—and their relatively high capital intensity explains the CD subsector's depressed ROCE. Conversely, despite more modest profitability levels as measured by EBITDA margins, the IO subsector requires less capital (including debt) to generate this profit level (i.e., it

Financial Analysis

Exhibit 41. ROCE

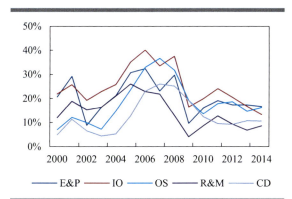

Note: E&P is exploration and production, IO is integrated oils, OS is oil field services, E&C is engineering and construction, R&M is refining and marketing, and CD is contract drilling.
Source: FactSet.

Exhibit 42. Capital Intensity (capex percentage of sales)

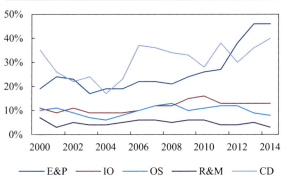

Note: E&P is exploration and production, IO is integrated oils, OS is oil field services, E&C is engineering and construction, R&M is refining and marketing, and CD is contract drilling.
Source: FactSet.

is relatively less capital intensive), which boosts their ROCE to the highest levels among all energy subsectors.

Finally, it is worth highlighting the E&P subsector in this context. Despite having continuously increasing capital intensity, which helps them yield the second-highest capital intensity in the industry (as shown in Exhibit 42), E&P companies can maintain a relatively high ROCE by generating the second-highest profitability (in terms of EBITDA margins) when using their capital in these highly capex-intensive projects.

VALUATION OF ENERGY STOCKS

In this guide, I make a distinction between absolute valuation methods, which attempt to assess the absolute or intrinsic value on an individual company, and relative market–based methods, which use price multiples to assess the company's value relative to its peers or its own price history. I highlight which of the widely used valuation tools are most commonly applied for each of the energy subsectors.

ABSOLUTE VALUATION

DCF-RELATED VALUATION METHODS

DCF (discounted cash flow) valuation methods determine a company's intrinsic value as the present value of its expected future cash flows. The classical DCF valuation discounts a company's future free cash flow stream to calculate the present value of a company or security.

DCF models can use two types of free cash flow to value a company. First is the cash flow that is available to the company's suppliers of debt and equity capital (i.e., free cash flow to the firm, or FCFF), which is discounted at the weighted average cost of capital (WACC) in the DCF valuation. Second is the cash flow that is only available to the company's common shareholders after all debt payments for interest and principal have been made (i.e., free cash flow to equity, or FCFE), which is discounted at the cost of equity in the DCF model.

The DCF valuation is a common valuation tool for individual energy companies—and all other industries—in all subsectors. Although FCFE and FCFF models are used for valuation in all energy subsectors, the relatively stable capital structure of integrated oil companies, with their fairly low level of gearing (see the discussion in Balance Sheet Structure), supports the use of FCFE models for DCF valuations in this subsector. In contrast, highly levered refining and drilling companies with fluctuating debt-to-equity capital structures often suffer from negative free cash flows to equity; therefore, FCFF models are more often applied for DCF valuations in these energy subsectors.

Modified versions of the typical DCF valuation are commonly used in the energy sector in order to calculate the net asset value (NAV) as a proxy for the company's intrinsic value. The NAV is derived from discounting the expected cash flows from the company's asset base—that is, the oil and gas reserves for E&P companies and the drilling fleets for contract drillers. The NAV discounts the asset-based cash flow stream, and the DCF valuation discounts the free cash flow generated at the company level. This difference is important because the NAV calculation discounts the asset-based cash flow stream with longer time horizons (30–40 years for exploration projects), which often do not generate cash flow at the company level over the shorter financial forecast period for a typical 10–15-year DCF valuation.

This NAV cash flow stream, which is generated from the company's asset base, is often comparable to the FCFF concept because it represents the free cash flow that is available to debt and equity owners of the company. Similar to a typical FCFF model for a DCF valuation, net debt and minority interests must still be deducted from the present value of an asset-based cash flow stream to derive the intrinsic equity value (or NAV) of the company that is available to common equity holders. Similar to the DCF-derived equity value per share, the NAV/share is then compared with the current share price to determine how the market is currently valuing the company relative to its underlying assets (i.e., oil and gas reserves or drilling fleet).

NAV OF E&P COMPANIES

NAV calculations are particularly important for E&P companies because they capture the potential value of long-term exploration projects, which are part of probable (2P) or even possible (3P) reserves owing to the higher uncertainty regarding their timing and success. Given the long-term investment cycle of E&P companies, these exploration projects generate cash outflows for capital investments only in the short term before they produce cash inflows further out in the future, which is usually not captured in the financial forecast period.

To capture the different risk levels of oil and gas reserves in an E&P company's asset base, the industry distinguishes three types of NAV: core NAV, unrisked NAV, and risked NAV.

The core NAV usually captures the value of a company's proved (developed and undeveloped) reserves (1P), which are reported by the company and can be recovered with a high degree of certainty. This NAV estimate is based on the free cash flows from fully producing out the company's year-end proved 1P reserves (i.e., all the reserves are produced until they are fully depleted). The level of annual oil and gas production forecasts depends on specific estimates for the initial production rate and the decline curves of each separate field in the company's 1P reserve base. Depending on a country's reporting requirements, some companies are also allowed to report probable reserves, in which case proved and probable 2P reserves are often used as a basis for the core NAV calculation.

In order to convert these volumetric forecasts into a future cash flow stream, oil and gas price forecasts—as well as the company's cost structure, fiscal regime, and tax position—are applied to the projected volumes. The projected cash flow stream from these 1P reserves is discounted at an after-tax discount rate of 10% to derive the net present value (NPV) of the company's oil and gas reserves. The cash flows from these 1P reserves belong to the equity and debt owners of the company;

therefore, net debt and other corporate cost items need to be deducted to derive the core NAV, which reflects the monetary value of the company's reserve base that is available to equity owners.

The core NAV is the most conservative estimate for an E&P company's reserve base because it does not consider any future exploration success or the company's likelihood of being a going concern. Instead, this so-called blowdown valuation simply assumes that the company's year-end proved reserves are fully produced out, and it takes into account only the future capital investment necessary to fully exploit the 1P reserve base. No exploration activities are considered to grow the future reserve base. The conservative core NAV value is seen as a valuation floor for the company and tends to be lower than the company's share price because the NAV value does not discount any future growth prospects.

Because the core NAV is based on the company's proved reserves, this reserve valuation is similar to the required SMOG calculation provided by the company under FAS 69, which also calculates a conservative blowdown calculation of the company's year-end proved reserves. The company's SMOG value, however, is based on historical commodity prices; therefore, the SMOG value appears to be more backward looking than a typical core NAV calculation.

The unrisked NAV takes into account the additional value generated by the development of exploration prospects from probable (2P) and possible (3P) reserves for which the likelihood of recovery is at least 10%. For so-called resource or exploration plays, the unrisked NAV can also include contingent resources, which fall into the category of subcommercial hydrocarbon accumulations that cannot be classified as reserves.

Not only does the unrisked NAV include more uncertain reserves from exploration prospects, but it is also based on the (rather unrealistic) assumption that all of these prospects yield a commercial hydrocarbon discovery. Thus, the unrisked NAV reflects the opposite extreme of the overly pessimistic core NAV; it describes the overly optimistic scenario of 100% exploration success on all targeted prospects. E&P companies tend to trade at a valuation discount to their unrisked NAV, which reflects the market's unwillingness to believe that all exploration efforts will be successful.

The risked NAV can be considered a realistic compromise between the overly pessimistic core NAV and the overly optimistic scenario of an unrisked NAV. The risked NAV attempts to remedy the fact that the success rate of exploration prospects has historically been much lower than 100% by applying a success rate of less than 100% to the unrisked value of an exploration prospect (thereby "risking" the value of a prospect). Considering that exploration success is a binary process (hydrocarbons are found or they are not), it could be argued that applying success probabilities to each prospect in an exploration portfolio must lead to incorrect valuation results. The risked NAV, however, provides a probability-weighted value for the whole exploration portfolio and captures the upside exploration potential on a risk-adjusted basis.

The risked value of the exploration portfolio consisting of probable (2P) and possible (3P) reserves as well as of contingent resources is then added to the core NAV for the proved (1P) reserves to derive the risked NAV for the total reserve base. The risked NAV provides the upside scenario for possible exploration success and gives an indication of how much exploration upside the market has already discounted in the current share price.

Exhibit 43 shows an example for the NAV calculation of Gulfport Energy Corporation (GPOR) in 2012. The NPV of the 1P reserves of $13.28 per share is

Exhibit 43. NAV for Gulfport Energy

2011 Proved Reserves	Proved Reserves				Probable & Possible Reserves						
	Volumes	US$ millions	USD/ Share		Unrisked Valuation				Risked Valuation		
Proved developed				Exploration Prospects	MM boe	US$ millions	USD/ share	Expected Success Rate	MM boe	US$ millions	USD/ Share
Oil (MM bl)	7.485	286	5.13	Grizzly Oil Sands	196	353	6.34	45%	88	159	2.85
Gas (bcf)	6.152	39	0.70	Gulf Coast	6	95	1.70	60%	4	57	1.02
Proved undeveloped				Niobrara Shale	15	105	1.89	30%	5	32	0.57
Oil (MM bl)	9.260	353	6.35	Utica Shale	410	4,305	77.35	35%	144	1,507	27.07
Gas (bcf)	9.576	61	1.09	Total	627	4,857	87.27	Total	240	1,754	31.51
Total proved reserves (MM boe)	19.37	739	13.28	Core NAV			13.91	Core NAV			13.91
				Unrisked NAV			101.18	Risked NAV			45.42
Debt and other items											
Diamondback Energy Investment		166	2.99								
Net debt		131	2.35								
Minority interests		0	0.00								
Net additions		35	0.63								
	Core NAV		13.91								

Note: MM bl is million barrels; bcf is billion cubic feet; bl is barrel; MM boe is million barrels of oil equivalent.
Sources: Author's illustration and calculation based on underlying data from company information.

calculated from proved (1P) reserves, which were reported by the company at the end of 2011. The proved reserve NPV is adjusted for net debt and GPOR's investment in Diamond Energy, resulting in a conservative core NAV of $13.91.

The probable (2P) and possible (3P) reserves reflect the upside potential from several exploration prospects. Under the (highly unrealistic) assumption that all prospects will be 100% successful, the unrisked NAV comes to $101.18 (core NAV of $13.91 plus total unrisked valuation of $87.27).

Assuming more realistic success rates for each exploration prospect (i.e., less than 100%), GPOR's risked NAV is estimated to be $45.42 (core NAV of $13.91 plus total risked valuation of $31.51). At the time of the valuation in November 2012, the stock was trading in the low $30 range, so the share price was already discounting some upside potential from exploration prospects, as reflected in the risked NAV—in particular, from the Utica Shale.

Just as for DCF calculations, every NAV valuation depends on the highly subjective choice of several input variables that will have a significant impact on the valuation's outcome. Therefore, it may be questionable to rely on a deterministic model for the NAV calculation, which only calculates *one* risked NAV value as a point estimate.

Instead, stochastic models can calculate a *range* or *distribution* of NAV values by running a large number of calculations or simulations from a defined range of input variables. In a Monte Carlo simulation, a different set of input variables from a previously defined range or distribution of input values is combined to calculate the NAV as an output variable. Based on a large number of iterations, the stochastic model also calculates a large number of possible NAV outputs and displays these results as an NAV probability distribution with an estimated mean NAV value and the most likely range of NAV outcomes.

The same NAV methodology can be applied to IO companies because these companies are characterized by a mixture of upstream exploration and production activities and downstream refining and marketing operations (and often petrochemical units).

Although the upstream division of an integrated oil company is valued with the same core and risked NAV concepts just described, the downstream refining and petrochemical units are valued separately, and their values are then added to the risked NAV of the E&P business (similar to the other assets or investments that also need to be considered in the company's total value).

The values of the company's refining and petrochemical assets can be calculated either as NPVs from a typical DCF valuation or by applying a market multiple (P/E or EV/EBITDA multiple) to the most current profit or operating profit of each division. Because it determines each of the divisional values separately (core NAV for E&P plus multiple- or DCF-based NPVs for refining and petrochemicals), the NAV calculation for an IO company can also be considered a sum-of-the-parts valuation.

NAV OF CONTRACT DRILLERS

The NAV calculation for a contract drilling company is similar to that for an E&P company in that it is also derived from discounting the projected cash flow stream that is generated from the company's asset base—i.e., its drilling fleet. The fleet value of a drilling company is defined as the NPV of the firm's rig portfolio, which is derived from the NPV calculations of all rigs based on their projected cash flow streams.

The cash flow stream for a single rig depends on the duration of its drilling contract, the contracted day rate, the rig's drilling days (expected rig utilization), and its operating costs and operating efficiency. The rig's cash flow is also affected by technology and rig age, the interest expense associated with financing the rig's purchase, as well as the salvage value at the end of the rig's useful life. The salvage value is also used as a value surrogate for rigs that are currently not operating but instead are idle in the rig fleet (i.e., cold stacked).

Again, the cash flow stream generated by the rig portfolio is comparable to the FCFF concept because it captures the cash flow that is available to the company's debt and equity owners. Debt holders represent a large share of a drilling company's ownership structure because the contract drilling subsector has the highest gearing level among energy companies. Therefore, the company's WACC is used to discount the cash flow stream to derive the fleet's NPV. Net debt is then deducted from the fleet's NPV to calculate the NAV available to the company's equity owners.

Exhibit 44 illustrates the NAV calculation for offshore driller Noble Corporation. Based on NPV valuations for all individual rigs, the table summarizes the NPVs for each rig category according to water depth (jack-up versus semisubmersible versus drillship). After deducting net debt and minority interests, which were taken from the company's 2014 balance sheet, the calculation results in an NAV per share of $16.85.

NAV calculations for a contract driller's existing rig fleet are based on known rig rates and contract durations. For the most part, new rigs are not built unless long-term contracts have been signed. Therefore, an NAV based on an existing fleet is comparable with the core NAV for E&P companies. In the event that a driller's NAV incorporates the future delivery of (speculative) newbuild rigs for which no leasing contracts have been signed and the rig rates are unknown, then the NAV becomes comparable with the risked NAV calculation for E&P companies, which tries to capture the upside potential of (highly uncertain) future exploration success.

Similar to the core NAVs of E&P companies, the NAVs for the contract drilling subsector can also be used to identify share price support levels. Although NAVs for contract drillers have, on average, been trading at a small valuation premium to their underlying share prices (an average price/NAV, or P/NAV, level of 115%, the P/NAV tends to provide support for falling share prices at P/NAV levels of 75%–80% during a downturn and, on the upside, the P/NAV ratio can reach 200%.

The variance of the P/NAV multiple depends on market sentiment for the contract drilling subsector in general and on the composition of each drilling company's fleet,

Exhibit 44. NAV for Offshore Driller Noble

Rig Type	Water Depth (feet)	No. of Rigs	Average Day Rate (US$)	NPV for Rig Type (US$ millions)
Premium jack-up	Shallow (300)	5	$91,000	$385
High-specification jack-up	Shallow (400–500)	10	$242,000	2,550
Semisubmersible	Mid, deep, and ultra deep (1,000–12,000)	9	$395,000	1,665
Drillship	Ultra deep (8,200–12,000)	8	$536,000	4,985
			NPV of drilling fleet (USD mn)	9,585
			Minus net debt (FY2014)	4,800
			Minus minority interests (FY2014)	722
			NAV	$4,063
			NAV/share	$16.58

Sources: Author's illustration and calculation based on underlying fleet data from company information.

as well as its exposure to the most prominent market segment during the drilling cycle (onshore, offshore shallow water, offshore, deepwater, and so forth).

DISCOUNTED DIVIDEND VALUATION

To calculate a company's intrinsic value, the discounted dividend valuation uses expected dividend payments as an alternative cash flow stream in the DCF model. Dividends are the relevant cash flow tool in a dividend discount valuation; therefore, a dividend discount model (DDM) is just another DCF model that is based on the FCFE concept. Thus, similar to a DCF model using cash flows to equity holders, the dividend discount valuation uses the company's respective cost of equity as the relevant discount rate.

Dividend discount valuations are commonly used as equity valuation tools for companies from all industry sectors. But within the energy sector, the DDM is most appropriate for integrated oil companies. Historically, the integrated oil subsector has reported one of the highest dividend payout ratios and has achieved the highest dividend yields (3%–5%) of all energy subsectors. The average payout ratio has been fairly stable at around 30% except during market downturns, when the payout ratio has briefly spiked because earnings collapsed while integrated oils maintained their dividend payments.

Therefore, the integrated oil subsector is considered a relative "safe haven" among energy companies, especially when industry downturns are accompanied by steep oil price declines. Integrated oils typically try to maintain their dividend payments, allowing them to deliver higher yields when share prices decline. When free cash flow comes under pressure during a period of prolonged oil price weakness, integrated oils cut their capex spending before they consider reducing their dividends. Thus, it was a fairly big deal when Eni cut its dividend after the financial crisis in 2009 and when BP suspended its dividend in the aftermath of the Macondo rig accident in the Gulf of Mexico in 2010.

Reliable dividend payments combined with attractive dividend yields are a major reason investors invest in integrated oil companies, given the subsector's uninspiring production and earnings growth rates. In fact, these growth rates frequently tend to fall short of management's guidance as well as investors' expectations. Considering the subsector's disappointing track record of generating growth, it is often suggested that integrated oil companies should focus on maximizing cash returns to shareholders via dividend payments (and share buybacks) instead of wasting capex on technically complex exploration projects that tend to suffer from cost overruns and deliver weak returns.

Considering the prevailing perception among investors that the integrated oil subsector delivers reliable dividend payments, a DDM using projected dividend payments appears to be a good valuation tool to estimate the intrinsic equity value of integrated oil companies. When comparing the market capitalization of large integrated oil companies with their estimated NPV derived from DDMs, there is a strong correlation between the year-end market capitalization of integrated oil companies and their respective year-end NPVs (calculated by discounting the projected dividend stream back to the same point in time).

MARKET-BASED VALUATION MULTIPLES

In addition to these absolute valuation tools, all of the most commonly used market-based valuation multiples are applicable to companies in the energy sector. These valuation multiples are useful to determine the stock's valuation relative to its peers and to the overall market as well as to compare the current valuation level with the stock's own valuation history. This guide highlights which valuation multiple is preferred for each energy subsector and provides the valuation range (based on one-year forward valuation multiples) for these subsectors.

In order to detect the market psychology toward energy stocks during the past three industry cycles (i.e., the past 15 years), I also analyze the energy sector valuation relative to the broader market (reflected by the MSCI World Index) and the relative valuation of each subsector compared with the MSCI Energy Index.

Since 2000, the energy sector has moved through three industry cycles, with steep Brent oil price declines in 2000–2001 (Brent oil fell by 49% between October 2000 and November 2001), in 2008 (75% decline between March and December 2008), and in 2014–2016 (76% drop between June 2014 and January 2016). Relative valuation multiples should help to detect whether the energy sector and its subsectors followed *cyclical* or *secular* valuation trends during these past industry cycles. A secular valuation means that the energy sector's relative valuation does not follow the sector's underlying industry (or oil price) cycle.

Appendix 7 summarizes the historical valuation multiples for each energy subsector from 2000 to 2014. All valuation multiples are calculated for each subsector, even for those multiples that are not commonly used for some of these subsectors. The subsectors consist of the same group of companies that were used as categories to aggregate the financial information in the Financial Analysis section. A full list of all subsector constituents can be found in Appendix 4. Based on these constituent companies, an equal-weighted sector index was created for each of the six energy subsectors, and valuation multiples were calculated for each index to analyze relative valuation trends among these energy subsectors.

P/E

There are a number of reasons that P/E is not the best measure of the relative value of capital-intensive companies in the energy sector. P/E is an earnings-based multiple, and the earnings per share (EPS) number is easily distorted because of differences in international accounting policies and tax rates. Furthermore, the bottom-line EPS number incorporates depreciation expense, which does not reflect the capex charged in the capital-intensive E&P and IO subsectors. Finally, the highly cyclical refining subsector tends to generate net losses when the industry cycle bottoms, which makes it difficult to use P/E multiples to establish a consistent historical valuation range over several past industry cycles.

Given P/E's easy calculation and intuitive interpretation, however, investors widely use P/E multiples in the energy sector, particularly for subsectors that were able to maintain positive EPS track records throughout previous industry cycles. Therefore, it can best be applied to IO companies with resilient earnings and to the E&C subsector, which has less volatile P/E multiples.

Exhibit 45 shows the one-year forward P/E multiples for the MSCI Energy Index as absolute multiples and relative to the broader market (MSCI World Index). **Exhibit 46** shows, for each of the energy subsector indexes, the volatility of their one-year forward P/E multiples over the whole 15-year time period, defined as the minimum, median, and maximum P/E multiple between 2000 and 2015.

The P/E multiple for the energy sector has not followed a cyclical trading pattern over the past 15 years that tracked the industry cycle over three oil price declines, despite the industry being cyclical. Instead, as Exhibit 45 shows, the energy sector has moved through a secular revaluation; the sector's absolute one-year forward P/E multiple and the sector's relative P/E premium compared with the MSCI World Index have both decreased to lower valuation levels, where they have remained for an extended period of time.

Exhibit 45.   MSCI Energy: One-Year Forward P/E

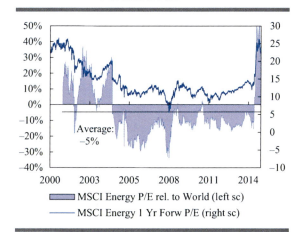

Source: FactSet.

Exhibit 46.   2000–15 P/E Volatility Subsectors

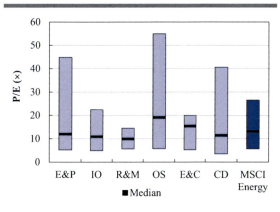

Source: FactSet.

The absolute P/E multiple contracted from 25× in 2000 to 11× in 2006, whereas the P/E difference from the broader market declined from a 30% premium in 2001 to a 30% relative valuation discount in 2006. Since then, the energy sector has persistently traded at lower absolute P/E multiples and at P/E discounts relative to the broader market until 2014–2015, when the P/E multiple expanded and the energy sector started to trade at a P/E premium to the MSCI World Index again.

The multiple expansion and valuation premium in 2014 and 2015 cannot be attributed to a significant share price increase of energy stocks; instead, index prices of the MSCI Energy Index dropped 30% between June 2014 and June 2015 in response to the significant oil price decline in the second half of 2014 and first half of 2015. As a result, one-year forward consensus EPS forecasts plunged even faster, leading to the significant spike in the one-year forward P/E multiple to 25×.

Considering that the relative valuation of the energy sector has moved on a secular basis during the past three oil price cycles, it would be misleading to take the energy sector's average P/E discount of 5% over the past 15 years as guidance for future valuation levels. Simply extrapolating the average P/E valuation discount for the past 15 years as an estimate into the future would most likely underestimate the energy sector's valuation discount relative to the MSCI World Index.

The volatility of one-year forward P/E multiples varied significantly between 2000 and 2015 at the subsector index level (see Exhibit 46). Over the past 15 years, the E&P, oil field services, and contract drilling subsectors experienced the biggest P/E multiple swings, whereas P/E valuations in the IO, E&C, and refining sectors were much less volatile. Therefore, P/E multiples are commonly applied to value companies in the IO and E&C subsectors.

Exhibit 47 and **Exhibit 48** show, for the IO and E&C subsector indexes, the historical P/E multiples as well as the P/E valuation premium or discount relative to the MSCI Energy Index benchmark.

The absolute P/E multiple valuation of the IO subsector in Exhibit 47 reflects the same secular revaluation pattern as in the MSCI World Energy Index (see Exhibit 45) because large-cap IOs make up the majority of the index constituents in the market-cap-weighted MSCI Energy Index. Similar to the MSCI World Energy Index, the absolute P/Es of IO subsector indexes have also persistently declined from 20× in 2000 to multiples below 10× between 2010 and 2014.

When analyzing the IO subsector's valuation relative to the MSCI Energy Index, I find that the P/E discount to the energy benchmark index has also consistently widened in a secular valuation trend from 2% in 2005 to 40% in 2015, which did not reflect the underlying oil price cyclicality during this time period. Therefore, the average 22% valuation discount over the past 15 years (see Exhibit 47) is probably a poor guide for the IO subsector's relative P/E valuation in the future because it would most likely underestimate the subsector's future valuation discount.

In contrast, the absolute and relative P/E valuations of the E&C subsector index in Exhibit 48 are moving on a cyclical basis; they simply reflect the underlying earnings (and oil price) cyclicality of this industry. The E&C subsector's relative P/E valuation has historically fluctuated in a one-standard-deviation valuation range between a 22% discount and a 40% premium to the P/E multiples of the MSCI Energy Index, which should reflect the upper and lower end of the subsector's valuation range relative to the MSCI Energy Index going forward.

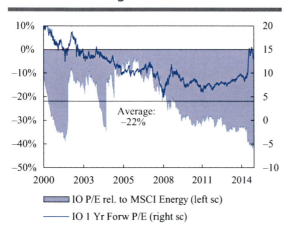

Exhibit 47. IO: One-Year Forward P/E Range

Source: FactSet.

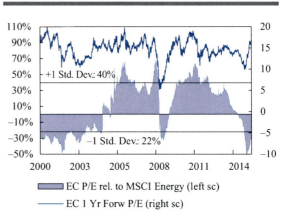

Exhibit 48. E&C: One-Year Forward P/E Range

Source: FactSet.

EV/EBITDA

Enterprise value (EV)/EBITDA is widely used as an important valuation multiple for energy companies because it remedies some of the P/E multiple shortcomings. EBITDA is often considered to be a very rough operating cash flow substitute to better compare earnings among different companies at the operating level instead of the after-tax net level.

The EV numerator of the EV/EBITDA multiple adds back net debt to the market capitalization; therefore, differences in the capital structure (equity versus debt levels) are not taken into account by this multiple, which compares how much operating cash flow is generated with the invested equity and debt capital. In the very capital-intensive energy industry with high gearing levels, EV-based multiples are more relevant than multiples that compare companies purely on ratios related to price or market capitalization (such as P/E). It is common to use an alternative cash flow number, such as debt-adjusted cash flow, instead of EBITDA in the denominator of this EV multiple.

Although EV/EBITDA is the most relevant multiple across all energy subsectors, it is replaced by the EV/EBITDAX multiple when comparing E&P companies. EBITDAX helps to eliminate accounting differences related to the treatment of exploration costs under FC and SE accounting. When comparing the EV/EBITDA multiples among all energy subsectors or with the valuation of the MSCI Energy Index, however, I use the EV/EBITDA multiple for the E&P subsector.

Exhibit 49 and **Exhibit 50** show the one-year forward EV/EBITDA multiples for the MSCI Energy Index on the left side and the 15-year volatility range of the EV/EBITDA multiples for each of the created energy subsector indexes on the right side.

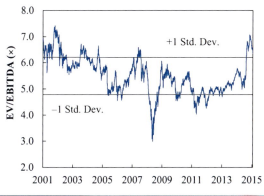

Exhibit 49. MSCI Energy: One-Year Forward EV/EBITDA

Source: FactSet.

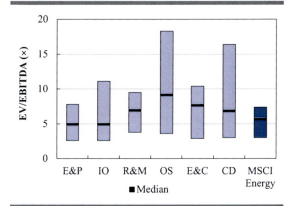

Exhibit 50. 2000–15 EV/EBITDA Volatility

Source: FactSet.

Over the past 15 years, the MSCI Energy Index has traded on average at a one-year forward EV/EBITDA multiple of 5.5× and within a fairly narrow trading range of 4.8× to 6.2× as defined by plus/minus one standard deviation from the long-term mean value. Although the index multiple fell to significantly lower levels during the 2008–09 financial crisis, it usually reversed very quickly after breaking through the lower end of this defined valuation range. For the first time since 2007, the EV/EBITDA multiple broke through the upper boundary in 2014 as the EBITDA forecasts decreased on the back of lower oil prices (the reasoning is the same as for the P/E described earlier).

The volatility of one-year forward EV/EBITDA multiples varies significantly between each of the created subsector indexes over the 15-year time period, with oil field services (OS) and contract drilling (CD) showing the largest dispersions. The median multiples over this entire time frame are also the highest for the OS subsector index (9.0×), followed by the E&C (7.5×) and the CD (6.0×) indexes. The IO and E&P indexes posted the lowest median multiples (4.8× for each) over the past 15 years. It is interesting to note that the volatility is higher for the IO index than for the E&P index during this time frame. Because the EV/EBITDA multiple is applicable to all energy subsectors, it is probably the most widely used valuation multiple. As a result, this guide provides the historical range of the one-year forward EV/EBITDA multiples for each of the created subsector indexes over the past 15 years. **Exhibits 51–56** give investors a good indication of the historical range of this important valuation metric for each subsector index.

Exhibit 51. E&P: One-Year Forward EV/EBITDA

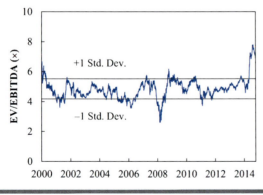

Source: FactSet.

Exhibit 52. IO: One-Year Forward EV/EBITDA

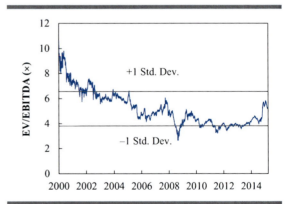

Source: FactSet.

Valuation of Energy Stocks

Exhibit 53. Refining: One-Year Forward EV/EBITDA

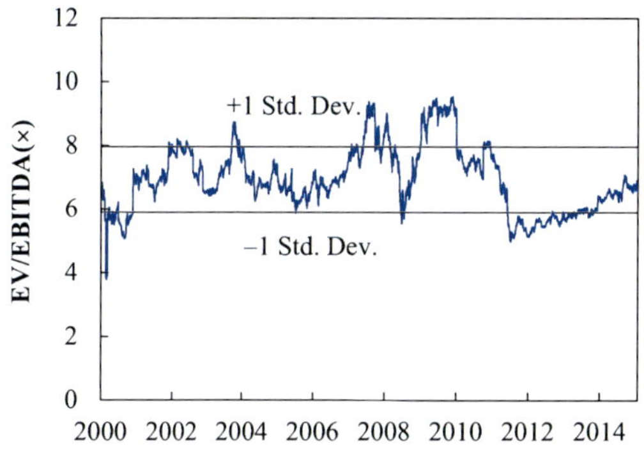

Exhibit 54. E&C: One-Year Forward EV/EBITDA

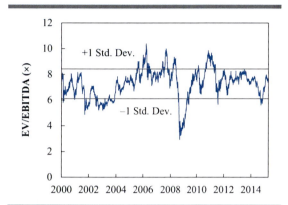

Source: FactSet.

Exhibit 55. OS: One-Year Forward EV/EBITDA

Source: FactSet.

Exhibit 56. CD: One-Year Forward EV/EBITDA

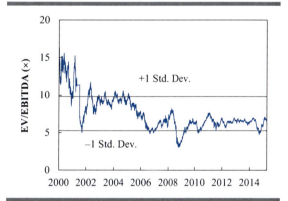

Source: FactSet.

PRICE/BOOK

Although EV/EBITDA is a widely used valuation multiple across all energy subsectors, this metric becomes impractical when companies report operating losses (negative EBITDA). In such instances, investors either have to move further up on the income statement and use an EV/sales multiple or abandon income-based multiples altogether and focus on balance sheet–related multiples, such as price/book (P/B). The P/B multiple is most usefully applied in the refining and marketing (R&M)

subsector because refining companies periodically realize operating losses during times of extreme volatility in product prices and operating margins.

Compared with other energy subsectors, the R&M index has traded, on average, at the lowest P/B multiple (1.3×) since 2000, closely followed by the CD subsector with an average P/B multiple of 1.4×. All other energy subsectors have traded at average P/B multiples closer to or above 2.0×, which is also reflected by the MSCI Energy's median index multiple of 1.9× since 2000 (see **Exhibit 57**).

The relatively low P/B value of the CD index can be attributed to this subsector's relatively low average return on equity (ROE) of 11%, which just covers the industry's assumed cost of equity of about 10%. In contrast, the R&M index seems to deserve a higher P/B multiple because this subsector has also achieved a higher average ROE (median of 16%) over the past 15 years, unless the market implies a higher cost of equity to R&M companies.

Although the basic relationship between P/B and ROE applies to energy companies (the market pays a higher P/B for higher ROEs), the *level* of this relationship differs within the energy sector between oil producers and refiners (E&P, IO, R&M) and their oil services providers (OS, E&C, CD). It appears that the market implies a higher cost of equity for the oil-producing and -refining segment because oil producers and refiners must achieve a higher ROE than oil services providers to get paid the same P/B multiple. **Exhibit 58** shows CD versus R&M and E&C versus IO. Therefore, the basic higher P/B for the higher ROE relationship is valid but applies for oil producers and refiners at higher ROE levels.

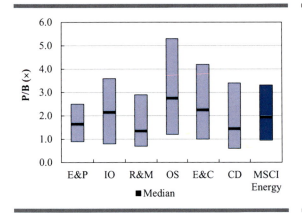

Exhibit 57. 2000–15 P/B Volatility

Source: FactSet.

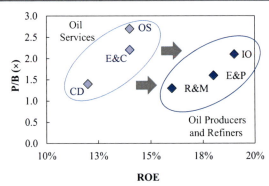

Exhibit 58. P/B vs. ROE for Subsectors

Source: FactSet.

The trading pattern for the two energy subsector indexes with the lowest average P/B multiples over the past 15 years is similar. As shown in **Exhibit 59** and **Exhibit 60**, the P/B multiples of the R&M and CD subsectors both reached values above the upper end of their respective trading range in the run-up to the financial crisis in 2008–2009. Since the share price corrections in 2008–2009, their P/B valuations have been stuck at the lower end of their trading range—at one-year forward multiples between 1.0× and 1.5×. The P/B of the CD subsector index has recently dropped below 1.0× as the buildup of overcapacity in the drilling industry has weighed on prices (rig rates) and has reduced earnings (and ROE) prospects in this subsector.

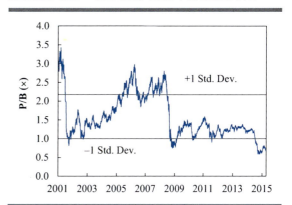

Exhibit 59. R&M: One-Year Forward P/B

Exhibit 60. CD: One-Year Forward P/B

Source: FactSet.

Source: FactSet.

DIVIDEND YIELD

Dividend yield as a relative valuation metric is based on the assumption that future dividend payments affect a company's value (as explained in the section on the DDM) and that expectations about a target yield can help determine the share price investors pay for these dividends. Two key requirements need to be met for the dividend yield to be used as a reliable valuation metric. First, dividend payments need to be stable and sustainable over the whole business cycle (although the payout ratio can fluctuate with the earnings cycle). Second, the dividend yield should also be range bound and not fluctuate too much. In other words, the dividend yield should be relatively predictable.

Just as the dividend discount valuation is best suited for IO companies, the dividend yield as a valuation metric is also best applied to this subsector. The IO subsector pays fairly stable and predictable dividends and has achieved the highest median dividend yield of 3.6% among all energy subsectors over the past 15 years. Since

2000, the dividend yield of the IO index has fluctuated between a low of 2.2% and a peak yield of 6.1% as shown in **Exhibit 61**.

Although the CD index has reached a higher peak dividend yield of 7.7%, it has also experienced the highest dividend volatility over the past 15 years, yielding only 0.1% at the low point. The high dividend volatility of the CD index can be attributed to payments of special dividends in some years, which are unsustainable over the long run and make it difficult to set target yields. In addition, companies in this sector have historically been more willing to reduce or even reset their regular dividends when industry conditions become more difficult.

Since 2000, the dividend yield for the IO subsector index has moved from the lower end of the long-term trading range (2.8%) to the upper end of the range (around 4.4%). The yield has stayed close to the top end of this range since 2010. In fact, over the past five years, the dividend yield of the IO subsector index has traded in a very narrow range of 4.0%–4.6% (shown in **Exhibit 62**). The fairly narrow dividend yield range makes it possible to set a target yield within this range to derive a price target based on expected dividend payments.

Exhibit 63 summarizes the one-year forward valuation multiples for each energy subsector by displaying the lowest, median, and highest multiple for each subsector over the 15 years between 2000 and 2015.

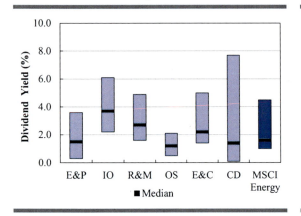

Exhibit 61. 2000–15 Dividend Yield Volatility

Source: FactSet.

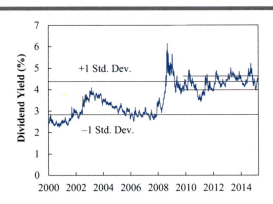

Exhibit 62. IO: One-Year Forward Dividend Yield

Source: FactSet.

Valuation of Energy Stocks

Exhibit 63. Valuation Summary: Low, Median, and High One-Year Forward Multiples, 2000–2015

One-Year Forward Multiples Range (2000–2014)	Exploration and Production	Integrated Oils	Refining and Marketing	Oil Field Services	Engineering and Construction	Contract Drilling
EV/Sales						
High	3.3×	2.7×	1.0×	3.3×	1.9×	5.7×
Median	0.9×	1.0×	0.6×	1.9×	1.3×	2.9×
Low	2.4×	0.5×	0.3×	1.0×	0.6×	1.5×
EV/EBITDA						
High	7.8×	11.1×	9.5×	18.3×	10.4×	16.4×
Median	4.8×	4.8×	6.8×	9.0×	7.5×	6.7×
Low	2.6×	2.6×	3.8×	3.6×	2.9×	3.0×
EV/EBIT						
High	30.2×	17.6×	13.8×	36.4×	15.0×	32.5×
Median	7.7×	6.6×	9.5×	12.9×	10.9×	9.9×
Low	3.7×	3.3×	6.0×	4.6×	3.8×	3.8×
P/E						
High	44.9×	22.5×	14.5×	55.0×	20.0×	40.6×
Median	11.5×	10.4×	9.4×	18.6×	14.9×	10.9×
Low	5.2×	4.9×	5.6×	5.7×	5.2×	3.5×
P/B						
High	2.5×	3.6×	2.9×	5.3×	4.2×	3.4×
Median	1.6×	2.1×	1.3×	2.7×	2.2×	1.4×
Low	0.9×	0.8×	0.7×	1.2×	1.0×	0.6×
Dividend yield						
High	3.6%	6.1%	4.9%	2.1%	5.0%	7.7%
Median	1.4%	3.6%	2.6%	1.1%	2.1%	1.3%
Low	0.3%	2.2%	1.6%	0.5%	1.4%	0.1%

Source: FactSet.

ENERGY SECTOR PERFORMANCE

In this final section, I analyze the share price performances at the energy sector level and for each subsector, in absolute terms as well as relative to a sector index and a broader market benchmark. The guide uses the MSCI World Energy Index as the relevant sector benchmark and the MSCI World Index to represent the broader market. Both of these benchmarks are market-capitalization-weighted indexes.

The six subsector indexes (E&P, IO, R&M, OS, E&C, and CD companies) consist of the same groups of companies that were used earlier to aggregate the financial information and valuation multiples. A full list of all subsector index constituents can be found in Appendix 4.

Each of these subsector indexes is created as an equal-weighted index rather than a market-cap-weighted index to eliminate the bias toward larger stocks in the index. This methodology also allows smaller index constituents to contribute proportionally at the subsector index level.

OUTPERFORMANCE SINCE 2000

Despite the share price declines in 2014 and 2015, the MSCI World Energy Index—when taking a long-term view since 2000—has strongly outperformed the broader market in absolute terms. Before falling oil prices led the energy benchmark index lower in the second half of 2014, the MSCI Energy Index had regained almost all of the losses it suffered in the aftermath of the 2008–09 financial crisis. By the end of June 2015, the MSCI Energy Index was still up 92% in absolute terms from its 2000 level, whereas the broader MSCI market index had only gained 25% over the past 15 years.

The MSCI Energy Index's relative performance is highly correlated with WTI oil prices as shown in **Exhibit 64** (correlation coefficient of 88%) because the price of oil is the underlying direct and indirect profit driver for all energy subsectors. An increase in relative performance shows periods when the energy sector outperformed, whereas declining periods reflect energy sector underperformance vis-à-vis the broader market. The recent oil price decline from $100/bbl to below $50/bbl beginning in June 2014 also explains the recent underperformance of the energy index relative to the broader market (which continued to increase during this period of oil price weakness).

The equal-weighted R&M index has benefited from strong refining margins during the acclaimed "golden age of refining"—that is, the time between 2004 and 2007 when global refining margins increased strongly owing to the favorable combination of growing demand and a supply shortfall based on insufficient refining capacity

Energy Sector Performance

Exhibit 64. Energy Relative to World vs. WTI Oil

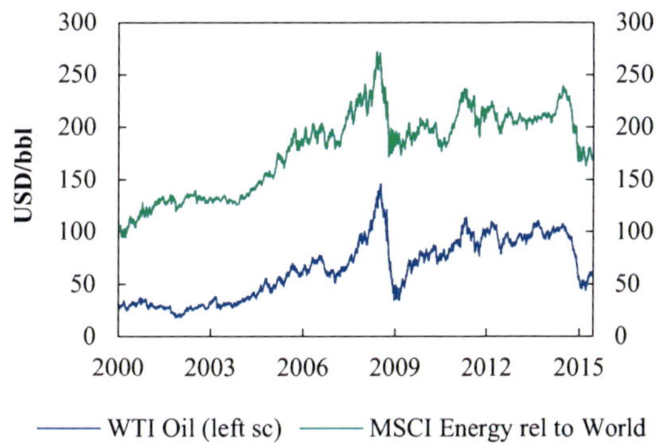

[Chart: WTI Oil (left sc) and MSCI Energy rel to World, 2000–2015, USD/bbl 0–300]

Source: FactSet.

after years of underinvestment in the industry. From 2010 onward, most US refiners have benefited from a wider-than-normal price spread between WTI and Brent oil prices (see Appendix 1 for the price spread). In fact, prior to this period, WTI typically traded at a premium to Brent. Subsequently, the sharp increase in US shale oil production has led to Brent trading at a premium to WTI.

Because US crude cannot be exported under the Jones Act, US refiners have access to a cheap source of domestic oil, although they can sell refined products into a global market at higher prices. Similarly, the E&P subsector index rallied on rising underlying oil prices until mid-2014. The sharp decline in oil prices that followed, however, has caused this subsector index to experience the steepest share price correction in the oil-producing and -refining segment.

Among the oil services providers, the E&C subsector index is the strongest-performing subsector since 2000, but it is still trailing its E&P and R&M peers in the oil-producing and -refining segment.

UNDERPERFORMANCE SINCE 2009

Although energy stocks have outperformed the broader market since 2000, the MSCI Energy Index has trailed the MSCI World Index since the end of the 2008–09 financial crisis. The MSCI Energy Index has gained 25% in absolute terms between 2009 and the end of June 2015, whereas the MSCI World Index has gained 90% over the same time period, benefiting from an extended period of monetary easing.

Energy stocks performed about in line with the broader market from 2009 until the end of 2012. In 2013, they started to underperform. The pace of their underperformance began to accelerate in 2014, when oil prices moved sharply lower. This underperformance continued in 2015. As a result, the relative performance of the MSCI Energy Index has deteriorated in line with underlying oil prices since the middle of 2014.

The relative performance of the energy subsectors has varied since the beginning of 2009. The following charts show the performances of each respective subsector relative to the energy sector's benchmark index, the MSCI Energy Index. Although the IO subsector has underperformed its energy peers in the oil-producing and -refining segment, the E&P and R&M subsector indexes have outperformed since the end of the financial crisis.

E&P companies have suffered the most because of the severe oil price decline since June 2014. In contrast, the R&M index, as shown in **Exhibit 65,** has benefited from lower oil prices, which reduces the feedstock costs in the refining process, and has extended its outperformance relative to the MSCI Energy Index.

The E&C subsector index, as shown in **Exhibit 66**, achieved the strongest relative outperformance in the first years after the financial crisis, but its relative performance stalled in 2012 and 2013, when the E&C industry was plagued by cost overruns and project delays owing to rising subcontracting costs and shortages for labor and materials.

As a result, the E&C index started to underperform even before the oil price decline weighed further on investor sentiment. Similarly, the relative sector underperformance of the CD index had already started at the end of 2013, when overcapacity in the onshore and offshore drilling markets pushed rig rates and profit expectations lower.

Exhibit 65. IO, R&M, and E&P Subsectors Relative to the MSCI Energy Index

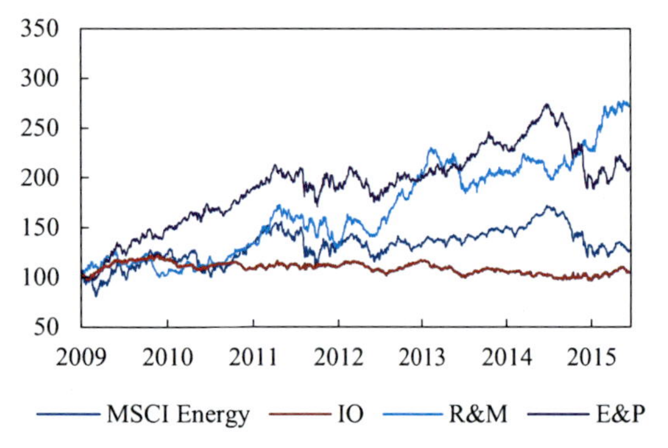

Exhibit 66. OS, E&C, and CD Subsectors Relative to the MSCI Energy Index

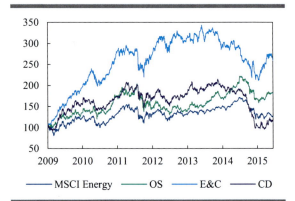

Source: FactSet.

RELATIVE SUBSECTOR PERFORMANCES

Finally, I will analyze how individual energy subsectors perform relative to their index peers in the energy sector based on changes in underlying commodity prices. Despite the strong correlation between oil prices and the relative performance of the MSCI Energy Index, not all energy subsectors included in the MSCI Energy Index react to oil price changes in a similar fashion.

Because the MSCI Energy Index is market-cap weighted, the index's relative performance is highly dependent on the effect that oil price changes have on the largest index constituents (i.e., IO companies). Therefore, the subsector indexes are created as equal-weighted indexes to eliminate the bias toward larger stocks in the index and to give the impact that oil prices have on smaller index constituents a proportionate contribution at the subsector index level.

The IO subsector is the most defensive of the energy subsectors because integrated oils are big cash flow–generating companies with solid balance sheets. Therefore, they tend to outperform relative to their energy peers when oil prices decline or during periods of so-called risk-off market sentiment. In contrast, OS companies represent a high-beta subsector in energy. They outperform during periods when oil prices increase as well as when market sentiment is "risk-on."

Exhibit 67 shows the performance of the IO index *relative* to the OS index and in comparison to the WTI oil price movement. When the relative performance chart rises, integrated oils outperform oil services. The opposite happens when the relative performance chart falls.

Given that the IO and OS subsectors have contrasting relative share price sensitivity to underlying oil prices and to prevailing market sentiment, the two subsectors provide a good hedge or pairs trade within the energy sector. When oil prices collapse (as in 2008–2009), the manager of a dedicated energy fund should buy (or go overweight) IO and sell (or go underweight) OS. In contrast, when oil prices increase (2009–2011), the opposite applies: Energy investors should buy OS and sell IO in order to outperform the broader energy market.

It is important to emphasize that this relative pairs trade applies only within the energy sector when a dedicated energy fund manager needs to be invested at all times in any of the energy subsectors. **Exhibit 68** shows the performance of the defensive IO subsector relative to the broader MSCI World Index.

Compared with the overall market, the defensive IO index no longer provides a good defense against falling oil prices because the relative IO performance more or less tracks the change in oil prices. Therefore, managers who do not have to be invested in energy stocks at all times should stay away from defensive IO companies during times of falling oil prices and instead invest in other industries that directly benefit from lower oil prices (such as airlines or automobiles).

Exhibit 67. IO Relative to OS vs. WTI Oil

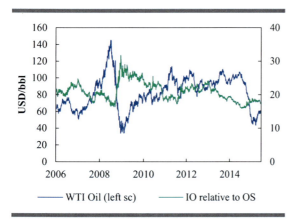

Source: FactSet.

Exhibit 68. IO Relative to MSCI World vs. WTI Oil

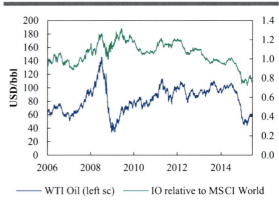

Source: FactSet.

A similar pairs trade between the E&P and R&M subsectors can be constructed within the energy space. Although both industries are considered high-beta energy subsectors, they have different exposures to underlying oil prices, such as WTI and Brent. Earnings and share prices of E&P companies are highly correlated with oil price movements, which inversely affect the feedstock costs of refiners (and thus refining profits if, for example, oil price increases cannot be fully passed on to customers through higher gasoline prices).

Exhibit 69 shows WTI oil price development against the performance of the E&P index *relative* to R&M index. When the relative performance chart rises, E&P companies outperform their R&M peers, and vice versa.

Given their contrasting relative share price exposure to the underlying oil price, the E&P and R&M subsectors provide another example for a good pairs trade within the energy sector. When oil prices surge (as in 2007–2008), the manager of a dedicated energy fund should buy (or go overweight) E&P companies but sell (or go underweight) R&M stocks. In contrast, when oil prices decline (2008–2009, 2012, or 2014–2015), the opposite applies and energy investors should overweight R&M and underweight E&P in order to beat the energy benchmark.

Finally, R&M companies in the United States, which have the operational flexibility to switch between WTI and Brent crude as feedstock for their refineries, can directly benefit when the price of WTI declines relative to Brent; as the WTI price discount widens, their operating costs decline. Therefore, the R&M index, which is heavily weighted toward US refiners, tends to outperform when the WTI–Brent price spread widens.

Energy Sector Performance

This tendency is shown in **Exhibit 70**, which compares the absolute performance of the R&M subsector index with the WTI–Brent price spread. Thus, when the WTI discount widens (as in 2011 or 2012–2013), energy fund managers should buy (or go overweight) R&M companies.

Exhibit 69. E&P Relative to R&M vs. WTI Oil

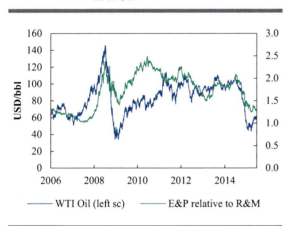

Source: FactSet.

Exhibit 70. R&M vs. WTI Discount to Brent

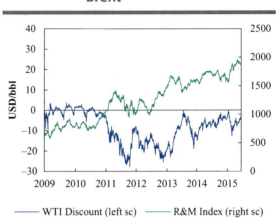

Source: FactSet.

INDUSTRY REFERENCES

BOOKS

- ***Petroleum Accounting: Principles, Procedures & Issues, 6th Edition**,* by Horace R. Brock, Martha Z. Carnes, and Randol Justice (2007)

    The authors provide a comprehensive overview of business operations and US financial accounting principles for exploration and production companies.

- ***The Petroleum Industry: A Nontechnical Guide,*** by Charles F. Conaway (1999)

    The author explains the basics of the oil and gas industry from exploration through refining. This book is useful for readers with limited or no knowledge of the oil industry in that it makes technical concepts easily understandable, but it is heavily focused on the exploration and production and oil services industries. The refining industry is explained only in the last 2 of 14 chapters.

- ***The Oil & Gas Industry: A Nontechnical Guide,*** by Joseph F. Hilyard (2012)

    This book is newer but similar to Charles Conaway's book. The author's intention is the same: to give an industry overview for industry outsiders with no petroleum engineering background. Although it is also mostly focused on upstream operations, it covers the midstream pipeline and downstream refining and trading industries in separate chapters.

- ***Fundamentals of Oil and Gas Accounting**,* **5th Edition,** by Charlotte J. Wright and Rebecca A. Gallun (2008)

    The authors provide a comprehensive overview of business activities and US financial accounting principles for exploration and production companies.

- ***The Prize: The Epic Quest for Oil, Money, and Power,*** by Daniel Yergin (1991)

    The author tells, in profound detail, the history of the global oil industry from the first well drilled in Pennsylvania in 1859 to Iraq's invasion into Kuwait in

1990 and analyzes how oil as a key energy source has influenced geopolitics and world affairs throughout the 20th century.

PERIODICALS

- ***Land Rig Newsletter*** (https://rigdata.com/land-rig-newsletter)

    This monthly publication focuses on current and long-term trends affecting the US and international onshore contract drilling industry.

- ***Offshore*** (www.offshore-mag.com)

    This monthly publication covers the key issues, trends, and technologies in the offshore E&P industry.

- ***Oil and Gas Investor*** (www.oilandgasinvestor.com)

    This monthly publication analyzes sector trends and provides news about the oil and gas industry as well as individual companies.

- ***Oil & Gas Journal*** (www.ogj.com)

    This weekly publication features articles on all aspects of the oil and gas value chain, including industry news, statistics, and editorial comments.

- ***Upstream*** (www.upstreamonline.com)

    This daily international oil and gas newspaper covers the E&P industry, reports company and geopolitical news, and analyzes technological developments in the industry.

- ***World Oil*** (www.worldoil.com)

    This monthly magazine covers news and industry developments related to all aspects of the upstream oil and gas industry (offshore, deepwater, subsea, shale, geology, drilling, completions, and production).

CFA Institute Industry Guides

RESEARCH AND DATA PROVIDERS

- **Baker Hughes Rig Count** (www.bakerhughes.com)

  This website provides free information for onshore rig counts (and offshore for the Gulf of Mexico) for North American rigs on a weekly basis and for international rigs on a monthly basis.

- **BP Statistical Review of World Energy** (www.bp.com/en/global/corporate/energy-economics/statistical-review-of-world-energy.html)

  The BP Statistical Review of World Energy is published annually by BP. It provides primary energy supply and demand data for all fuels (oil, gas, coal, nuclear, and renewables), including historical data over the past 20–25 years (depending on the fuel) and fuel-specific projections over the next 20 years.

- **ExxonMobil Outlook for Energy** (http://corporate.exxonmobil.com/en/energy/energy-outlook)

  "The Outlook for Energy" is published annually by ExxonMobil. It provides fuel-specific primary energy supply and demand information, including historical data and fuel-specific projections over the next 25 years.

- **Energy Intelligence** (www.energyintel.com)

  This research website provides news, data, and analysis services relating to global energy topics and developments. It also publishes daily and weekly newsletters as well as special reports.

- **IHS Global Insight** (www.ihs.com)

  IHS is a global research and consulting firm that provides economic and industry data, forecasts, and analyses related to a variety of sectors, including the oil and gas, energy equipment, and energy services sectors.

- **IHS ODS-Petrodata** (https://login.ods-petrodata.com)

  ODS-Petrodata provides weekly and monthly updates for global offshore rig market data and forecasts.

- **Platts** (www.platts.com)

  As part of McGraw Hill Financial, Platts provides news and analysis across all energy sectors (oil, gas, electric power, coal, and petrochemicals). Its

Industry References

services include market data and research reports relating to all energy market segments.

- **RigData** (www.rigdata.com)

  RigData provides weekly updated online data about industry trends, rig count, rig utilization, and day rates relating to the onshore and offshore drilling markets. It also publishes daily and weekly drilling permits by state and federal authorities. It publishes the *Land Rig Newsletter*.

- **Rigzone** (www.rigzone.com)

  Rigzone is an online provider of news, data, and market research services related to the offshore oil and gas industry.

- **Rystad Energy** (www.rystadenergy.com)

  Rystad Energy is an independent oil and gas consulting and business intelligence data firm offering global E&P and oil field services databases, research products, and strategy consulting.

- **Wood Mackenzie** (www.woodmac.com)

  Wood Mackenzie is a research and consulting firm that provides data, research, and consulting services about the global energy, metals, and mining industries.

GOVERNMENTAL AND INTERNATIONAL AGENCIES

- **Energy Information Administration** (www.eia.gov)

  The US Energy Information Administration site contains historical statistics, forecasts, and analyses on domestic and international primary energy supply and demand and prices.

- **International Energy Agency** (www.iea.org)

  The International Energy Agency (IEA) acts as an energy policy adviser to its 29 member countries and conducts a broad program of energy research, data compilation, and publications. Similar to BP and ExxonMobil, the IEA publishes an annual *World Energy Outlook* containing fuel-specific long-term supply and demand forecasts. It also issues a monthly *Oil Market Report*.

- **Organization of the Petroleum Exporting Countries** (www.opec.org)

    The Organization of the Petroleum Exporting Countries (OPEC) coordinates the petroleum policies of its oil-producing member countries to ensure the stabilization of international oil prices and to secure an efficient and regular global oil supply. On an annual basis, OPEC publishes its *World Oil Outlook*, which contains oil supply and demand projections for the next 25 years.

TRADE ASSOCIATIONS AND INDUSTRY TRAINING

- **American Gas Association** (www.aga.org)

    The American Gas Association (AGA) is a trade organization consisting of about 300 natural gas distribution, transmission, gathering, and marketing companies in North America. AGA members account for more than 90% of the natural gas delivered in the United States. AGA acts as a clearinghouse for gas energy information and represents the member companies in technical and energy policy matters.

- **American Petroleum Institute** (www.api.org)

    The American Petroleum Institute (API) is the petroleum industry's primary US trade association with member companies representing all energy subsectors, including exploration and production, transportation, and refining and marketing. The API provides public policy development, advocacy, research, and technical services as well as weekly estimates for crude oil and refined product inventory levels in the United States. The API also developed the "API gravity" measure for crude oil, which categorizes how "heavy" or "light" a crude oil is compared with water.

- **Colorado School of Mines** (www.mines.edu)

    Every July, the Colorado School of Mines Department of Petroleum Engineering offers a comprehensive three-week practical training workshop called "Petroleum SuperSchool" (http://csmspace.com/events/superschool), which is designed for professionals with a nonpetroleum engineering background, for nontechnical management personnel in energy firms, and for financial professionals interested in the oil and gas industry. The workshop is taught in a combination of classroom courses, real-world field trips, and hands-on experience in the department's state-of-the-art computer lab to solve authentic problems in small groups.

- **Energy Institute** (www.energyinst.org)

The Energy Institute is a chartered professional membership body that provides technical and scientific knowledge resources and professional development opportunities to individuals working in the energy industry and to 250 member companies worldwide.

- **Independent Petroleum Association of America** (www.ipaa.org)

The Independent Petroleum Association of America (IPAA) represents independent oil and gas producers and oil services companies across the United States. It advocates its members' views before the US Congress and federal agencies. IPAA provides economic and statistical information about the exploration and production industry in the United States.

- **International Association of Drilling Contractors** (www.iadc.org)

The International Association of Drilling Contractors (IADC) represents the worldwide oil and gas drilling industry. Oil and gas producers and oil field services suppliers can also become members. IADC offers print and electronic technical publications as well as training seminars to improve education and communication within the upstream petroleum industry.

- **International Association of Oil & Gas Producers** (www.iogp.org)

The International Association of Oil & Gas Producers represents national and international oil and gas companies in the upstream industry, which combine to produce more than half of the world's oil and more than one-third of its gas.

APPENDIX 1. AVERAGE ANNUAL REFERENCE PRICES

Average Annual Prices	2005	2006	2007	2008	2009	2010	2011	2012	2013	2014
Crude oil										
WTI crude oil (USD/bbl)	56.6	66.1	72.3	99.5	61.8	79.5	95.1	94.2	98.0	92.9
Brent crude oil (USD/bbl)	55.1	66.2	72.5	98.5	62.3	80.2	111.0	111.8	108.7	99.7
WTI premium/discount to Brent	1.49	−0.06	−0.15	1.07	−0.49	−0.73	−15.87	−17.59	−10.75	−6.85
Urals crude oil (CIF MED USD/bbl)	50.5	61.0	69.6	93.9	60.9	78.3	109.7	110.7	108.3	97.9
Indonesia Minas crude oil (USD/bbl)	54.0	65.1	73.6	100.2	64.1	81.7	113.2	115.1	108.4	98.1
Dubai crude oil (USD/bbl)	49.4	61.5	68.4	93.5	61.8	78.2	106.2	109.1	105.5	96.6
Natural gas										
Natural gas (NYM USD/mmbtu)	9.01	7.04	7.12	8.90	4.17	4.39	4.04	2.86	3.75	4.26
UK Natural Gas NBP (UK pence/thm)	45.7	53.7	30.7	63.3	37.2	41.4	58.3	59.2	66.9	51.1
Complex refining margins										
3:2:1 US Gulf Coast refining margin (USD/bbl)	11.43	10.92	13.97	10.02	8.80	9.94	25.11	29.34	23.50	19.07
3:2:1 Northwest Europe refining margin (USD/bbl)	10.11	10.37	11.67	10.27	8.83	8.62	7.94	11.78	9.61	10.28
Refined products										
Gasoline RBOB LA (USD/gal)	1.77	2.06	2.28	2.63	1.84	2.21	2.89	3.03	2.92	2.67
Gasoline conventional regular NY harbor (USD/gal)	1.56	1.82	2.05	2.45	1.66	2.10	2.79	2.93	2.81	2.61
Diesel no. 2 low sulfur NY harbor (USD/gal)	2.93	2.76	2.14	2.97	1.70	2.20	3.01	3.11	3.01	2.80
Jet fuel kerosene US Gulf Coast (USD/gal)	1.71	1.92	2.12	2.96	1.66	2.15	2.99	3.06	2.92	2.70
Euro jet kerosene near term (USD/tonne)						748	1,016	1,026	989	911

(continued)

Appendix 1. Average Annual Reference Prices

Average Annual Prices	2005	2006	2007	2008	2009	2010	2011	2012	2013	2014
Jet kerosene Singapore (USD/bbl)	67.8	80.7	86.7	121.2	70.0	90.2	125.6	126.7	122.9	112.4
Heating oil no. 2 NY harbor (USD/gal)	1.62	1.80	2.02	2.85	1.64	2.13	2.94	3.02	2.93	2.69
European gasoil (USD/tonne)					618	674	933	953	919	841

Notes: CIF MED is cost, insurance, and freight Mediterranean; NYM is the New York Mercantile Exchange; mmbtu is 1 million British thermal units; NBP is national balancing point; thm is therm; RBOB is reformulated blendstock for oxygen blending; LA is Los Angeles; and NY is New York City.
Source: FactSet.

APPENDIX 2. MONTHLY BAKER HUGHES RIG COUNT

	2005	2006	2007	2008	2009	2010	2011	2012	2013	2014	2015
Total global rig count											
January	2,665	3,038	3,254	3,296	2,974	2,773	3,436	3,751	3,539	3,598	3,309
February	2,745	3,133	3,352	3,417	2,753	2,982	3,536	3,900	3,679	3,736	2,986
March	2,617	3,069	3,135	3,259	2,313	2,879	3,434	3,663	3,488	3,597	2,557
April	2,415	2,707	2,836	3,009	2,055	2,676	3,103	3,298	3,209	3,388	2,268
May	2,485	2,795	2,862	3,073	1,983	2,750	3,130	3,335	3,178	3,371	2,127
June	2,580	2,979	2,996	3,269	1,987	2,859	3,257	3,484	3,277	3,445	2,136
July	2,759	3,155	3,144	3,436	2,080	3,032	3,397	3,516	3,362	3,608	2,167
August	2,894	3,174	3,156	3,523	2,105	3,127	3,613	3,490	3,416	3,642	2,226
September	2,856	3,134	3,166	3,557	2,203	3,122	3,662	3,468	3,431	3,659	2,171
October	2,923	3,130	3,124	3,518	2,271	3,165	3,722	3,458	3,437	3,657	2,086
November	3,021	3,077	3,161	3,448	2,409	3,233	3,683	3,461	3,452	3,670	2,047
December	2,993	3,125	3,207	3,221	2,509	3,227	3,612	3,390	3,478	3,570	1,969
North American rig count											
January	1,805	2,133	2,282	2,243	1,930	1,726	2,275	2,580	2,260	2,273	2,051
February	1,869	2,248	2,371	2,385	1,733	1,914	2,347	2,696	2,404	2,395	1,711
March	1,726	2,171	2,141	2,205	1,301	1,805	2,287	2,471	2,220	2,252	1,306
April	1,517	1,795	1,852	1,935	1,069	1,602	1,974	2,120	1,908	2,039	1,066
May	1,566	1,875	1,855	1,998	990	1,660	1,979	2,110	1,895	2,021	969
June	1,648	2,073	1,981	2,167	1,020	1,760	2,099	2,199	1,944	2,101	990
July	1,848	2,234	2,126	2,344	1,106	1,923	2,247	2,252	2,057	2,226	1,089
August	1,980	2,220	2,147	2,436	1,158	2,025	2,430	2,229	2,149	2,303	1,073
September	1,949	2,185	2,134	2,449	1,217	2,002	2,488	2,214	2,147	2,336	1,014
October	2,020	2,165	2,100	2,422	1,288	2,066	2,525	2,199	2,122	2,349	966
November	2,086	2,138	2,169	2,352	1,384	2,103	2,498	2,194	2,141	2,346	928
December	2,045	2,174	2,171	2,143	1,485	2,109	2,432	2,137	2,143	2,257	826

(continued)

Appendix 2. Monthly Baker Hughes Rig Count

	2005	2006	2007	2008	2009	2010	2011	2012	2013	2014	2015
International rig count											
January	860	905	972	1,053	1,044	1,047	1,161	1,171	1,279	1,325	1,258
February	876	885	981	1,032	1,020	1,068	1,189	1,204	1,275	1,341	1,275
March	891	898	994	1,054	1,012	1,074	1,147	1,192	1,268	1,345	1,251
April	898	912	984	1,074	986	1,074	1,129	1,178	1,301	1,349	1,202
May	919	920	1,007	1,075	993	1,090	1,151	1,225	1,283	1,350	1,158
June	932	906	1,015	1,102	967	1,099	1,158	1,285	1,333	1,344	1,146
July	911	921	1,018	1,092	974	1,109	1,150	1,264	1,305	1,382	1,118
August	914	954	1,009	1,087	947	1,102	1,183	1,261	1,267	1,339	1,137
September	907	949	1,032	1,108	986	1,120	1,174	1,254	1,284	1,323	1,140
October	903	965	1,024	1,096	983	1,099	1,197	1,259	1,315	1,308	1,111
November	935	939	992	1,096	1,025	1,130	1,185	1,267	1,311	1,324	1,109
December	948	951	1,036	1,078	1,024	1,118	1,180	1,253	1,335	1,313	1,095
US oil rig count											
January	185	237	255	318	309	444	809	1,225	1,315	1,422	1,223
February	189	219	278	337	260	456	783	1,265	1,329	1,430	986
March	178	253	271	350	217	489	851	1,318	1,354	1,487	813
April	169	254	283	360	202	513	926	1,328	1,381	1,534	703
May	148	265	287	390	187	555	958	1,383	1,410	1,536	646
June	149	302	281	375	219	583	1,003	1,421	1,390	1,558	628
July	189	302	296	393	261	603	1,025	1,416	1,401	1,562	664
August	220	315	300	416	286	672	1,069	1,419	1,388	1,575	675
September	203	295	311	423	297	673	1,060	1,410	1,362	1,592	640
October	227	289	326	408	330	696	1,078	1,408	1,357	1,582	578
November	275	297	354	412	379	724	1,130	1,386	1,391	1,572	555
December	235	278	325	364	418	765	1,193	1,327	1,382	1,499	538
US gas rig count											
January	1,069	1,247	1,440	1,422	1,150	861	913	777	434	358	319
February	1,090	1,322	1,472	1,418	970	905	906	710	428	335	280
March	1,152	1,321	1,472	1,447	810	941	880	658	389	318	233
April	1,156	1,353	1,460	1,473	742	958	882	613	366	323	225
May	1,183	1,381	1,471	1,479	703	967	881	594	354	326	225
June	1,219	1,359	1,489	1,530	687	958	873	534	353	314	228

(continued)

	2005	2006	2007	2008	2009	2010	2011	2012	2013	2014	2015
July	1,221	1,408	1,474	1,555	677	972	877	505	369	318	209
August	1,220	1,436	1,523	1,606	699	973	898	473	380	338	202
September	1,273	1,445	1,443	1,559	710	967	923	435	376	338	197
October	1,247	1,450	1,428	1,552	728	967	934	416	376	346	197
November	1,212	1,395	1,463	1,443	748	953	865	424	367	344	189
December	1,234	1,425	1,452	1,347	759	919	809	431	374	340	162

Source: Baker Hughes.

APPENDIX 3. US COMPANIES USING SUCCESSFUL EFFORTS VS. FULL-COST ACCOUNTING

Successful Efforts Accounting	Full-Cost Accounting
Anadarko Petroleum	Abraxas Petroleum
Antero Resources	Apache Corporation
Bill Barrett Corporation	Callon Petroleum
Bonanza Creek Energy	Carrizo Oil & Gas
Cabot Oil & Gas	Chesapeake Energy
Chevron	Cimarex Energy
Clayton Williams Energy	Devon Energy
Concho Resources	Energy XXI
ConocoPhillips	EXCO Resources
Continental Resources	Gulfport Energy
Eclipse Energy	Halcón Resources
EOG Resources	Matador Resources
EQT Corporation	Newfield Exploration
Erin Energy	Resolute Energy
ExxonMobil	Rosetta Resources
Goodrich Petroleum	SandRidge Energy
Hess Corporation	Southwestern Energy
Magnum Hunter Resources	Stone Energy Corporation
Marathon Oil	Triangle Petroleum
Noble Energy	Ultra Petroleum
Oasis Petroleum	Unit Corporation
Occidental Petroleum	
Panhandle Oil and Gas	
Par Petroleum	
PDC Energy	
Penn Virginia Corporation	
Pioneer Natural Resources	
Range Resources	
Whiting Petroleum	

Source: Company information, as of FY2014.

APPENDIX 4. ENERGY SUBSECTOR CONSTITUENTS

Exploration and Production	Integrated Oils	Refining and Marketing	Oil Field Services	Engineering and Construction	Contract Drilling
US successful efforts	BP	Caltex Australia	Baker Hughes	CGG	Atwood Oceanics
Anadarko Petroleum	Chevron	Hellenic Petroleum	Cameron International	FMC Technologies	China Oilfield Services
Cabot Oil & Gas	China Petroleum & Chemical Corp.	HollyFrontier	CARBO Ceramics	Fugro	Diamond Offshore Drilling
ConocoPhillips	Eni	Indian Oil Corp.	Halliburton	John Wood Group	Ensco
EOG Resources	Exxon Mobil	Neste Oil	Key Energy Services	Oceaneering International	Ensign Energy Services
EQT Corporation	Gazprom	PTT Public	National Oilwell Varco	Offshore Oil Engineering	Fred.Olsen Energy
Hess Corporation	Lukoil	Reliance Industries	Schlumberger	Petrofac	Helmerich & Payne
Marathon Oil	OMV	Saras	Superior Energy Services	Saipem	Nabors
Noble Energy	Petrobras	SK Holdings	Total Energy Services	SapuraKencana Petroleum	Noble Corp.
Occidental Petroleum	PetroChina	S-Oil	Trican Well Service	SBM Offshore	Parker Drilling
Pioneer Natural Resources	Repsol	Tesoro	Weatherford	Sembcorp Marine	Patterson-UTI Energy
Range Resources	Royal Dutch Shell	Valero		Subsea 7	Precision Drilling
	Statoil	Western Refining		Technip	Rowan
US full cost	Suncor			Tenaris	Seadrill
Apache Corporation	Total			TGS-NOPEC Geophysical	Transocean
Callon Petroleum					
Carrizo Oil & Gas					
Chesapeake Energy					

(continued)

Appendix 4. Energy Subsector Constituents

Exploration and Production	Integrated Oils	Refining and Marketing	Oil Field Services	Engineering and Construction	Contract Drilling
Cimarex Energy					
Devon Energy					
Gulfport Energy					
Newfield Exploration					
Southwestern Energy					
Ultra Petroleum					
International					
Canadian Natural Resources					
China National Offshore Oil Corp.					
DNO ASA					
Encana Corp.					
Lundin Petroleum					
OAO Tatneft					
Oil and Natural Gas Corp.					
Oil Search					
Premier Oil					
PTT Exploration & Production					
Santos Limited					
Tullow Oil					
Vermilion Energy					
Woodside Petroleum					

Sources: Author's energy subsector classification based on FactSet financial data and on company information.

APPENDIX 5. BALANCE SHEET STRUCTURE OF ENERGY SUBSECTORS

	2005	2006	2007	2008	2009	2010	2011	2012	2013	2014	Average
Cash (percentage of total assets)											
Exploration and production											
US successful efforts	4%	2%	2%	3%	3%	6%	5%	3%	5%	8%	3%
US full cost	5	2	2	6	4	4	6	5	5	7	4
International	13	9	13	16	12	11	12	12	8	9	12
Integrated oils	6	6	5	5	4	5	5	4	5	6	5
Refining	13	14	14	15	12	13	14	10	10	10	12
Oil field services	12	14	11	10	13	10	8	8	9	9	10
Engineering and construction	19	21	17	19	19	15	12	12	11	11	13
Contract drilling	11	10	14	8	8	9	9	13	10	9	10
Net PP&E (percentage of total assets)											
Exploration and production											
US successful efforts	57%	63%	61%	68	67%	64%	68%	72%	73%	72%	66%
US full cost	76	81	82	80	78	80	80	81	81	81	79
International	61	53	50	56	55	57	58	55	59	55	56
Integrated oils	63	60	55	60	61	61	63	66	68	68	63
Refining	39	38	35	37	36	35	33	36	38	42	38
Oil field services	22	23	27	27	27	26	26	27	27	27	25
Engineering and construction	29	26	27	29	33	35	35	33	35	38	32
Contract drilling	66	67	63	68	70	70	71	69	71	73	68
Shareholders' equity (percentage of total assets)											
Exploration and production											
US successful efforts	47%	46%	47%	45%	46%	47%	47%	47%	50%	49%	45%
US full cost	49	50	50	49	49	51	50	46	48	46	47

(continued)

Appendix 5. Balance Sheet Structure of Energy Subsectors

	2005	2006	2007	2008	2009	2010	2011	2012	2013	2014	Average
International	61	53	52	58	54	53	55	57	56	53	55
Integrated oils	60	61	61	64	63	65	65	65	65	63	62
Refining	40	39	42	37	37	37	38	40	40	39	35
Oil field services	52	51	55	54	57	60	57	57	56	55	51
Engineering and construction	41	38	38	40	46	47	53	51	52	51	42
Contract drilling	63	57	54	44	49	50	49	48	50	50	54
Net gearing (net debt to equity)											
Exploration and production											
US successful efforts	22%	38%	28%	34%	34%	23%	28%	35%	27%	23%	38%
US full cost	32	40	42	42	49	40	32	47	42	43	51
International	–10	–8	–17	–18	–6	–4	–6	–4	5	11	–2
Integrated oils	20	19	21	19	22	16	15	15	16	19	19
Refining	51	50	36	70	64	61	44	51	54	62	73
Oil field services	14	11	15	16	12	13	18	21	21	22	26
Engineering and construction	–4	0	10	1	–4	4	5	15	14	18	16
Contract drilling	14	27	31	76	62	55	59	51	50	51	41
Current ratio											
Exploration and production											
US successful efforts	1.1×	1.1×	1.0×	1.1×	1.2×	1.4×	1.2×	1.3×	1.3×	1.4×	1.2×
US full cost	1.3×	1.0×	1.0×	1.2×	1.3×	1.1×	1.1×	1.2×	1.3×	1.3×	1.2×
International	2.2×	1.6×	1.6×	1.9×	1.7×	1.5×	1.5×	1.9×	1.7×	1.6×	1.7×
Integrated oils	2.1×	2.2×	1.9×	1.9×	1.8×	1.7×	1.7×	1.6×	1.8×	1.8×	1.8×
Refining	2.0×	1.9×	1.7×	2.1×	2.0×	2.0×	1.9×	1.8×	1.8×	1.8×	1.9×
Oil field services	2.2×	2.2×	2.3×	2.3×	2.7×	2.6×	2.5×	2.6×	2.5×	2.3×	2.2×
Engineering and construction	1.4×	1.5×	1.5×	1.5×	1.5×	1.5×	1.4×	1.6×	1.5×	1.5×	1.4×
Contract drilling	2.6×	2.2×	2.9×	2.7×	2.5×	2.6×	2.4×	2.6×	2.0×	2.0×	2.6×

Notes: Please see Appendix 4 for a list of the companies included in each energy subsector. PP&E is property, plant, and equipment.
Source: FactSet.

APPENDIX 6. FINANCIAL INDICATORS RELATED TO THE INCOME STATEMENT

	2005	2006	2007	2008	2009	2010	2011	2012	2013	2014	Average
Exploration and production											
Sales growth	44%	20%	0%	34%	–34%	18%	18%	–21%	–18%	6%	17%
EBITDA margin	27%	31%	32%	31%	27%	29%	29%	37%	49%	49%	31%
EBIT margin	20%	23%	22%	23%	12%	17%	18%	22%	29%	28%	20%
Net margin	13%	16%	14%	14%	6%	12%	12%	16%	18%	18%	13%
Capex (% of sales)	19%	22%	22%	21%	24%	26%	27%	38%	46%	46%	26%
Dividend payout[a]	11%	12%	15%	13%	52%	24%	23%	22%	26%	28%	23%
EBIT interest coverage	17.1×	19.3×	10.5×	16.0×	5.1×	8.4×	10.6×	9.4×	9.3×	9.4×	10.1×
ROE[b]	26%	28%	20%	24%	7%	14%	15%	15%	14%	14%	18%
ROCE[b]	31%	32%	23%	30%	10%	16%	19%	17%	17%	17%	21%
Integrated oils											
Sales growth	16%	20%	5%	26%	–25%	22%	26%	9%	2%	–7%	15%
EBITDA margin	21%	21%	20%	20%	17%	17%	17%	16%	14%	14%	18%
EBIT margin	16%	17%	16%	16%	11%	12%	13%	11%	9%	8%	13%
Net margin	9%	10%	11%	9%	6%	8%	9%	7%	7%	5%	8%
Capex (% of sales)	9%	10%	12%	12%	15%	16%	13%	13%	13%	13%	12%
Dividend payout[a]	21%	20%	20%	20%	43%	26%	19%	23%	25%	34%	25%
EBIT interest coverage	32.8×	28.1×	16.8×	26.6×	15.4×	14.6×	16.2×	10.6×	12.2×	9.1×	17.1×
ROE[b]	23%	27%	25%	25%	11%	17%	20%	16%	14%	11%	19%
ROCE[b]	35%	40%	34%	38%	16%	20%	24%	21%	17%	13%	25%
Refining and marketing											
Sales growth	34%	25%	20%	19%	–14%	13%	20%	27%	0%	2%	20%
EBITDA margin	10%	9%	9%	6%	4%	6%	7%	5%	4%	5%	7%
EBIT margin	8%	7%	7%	4%	2%	3%	4%	3%	2%	2%	5%
Net margin	5%	5%	5%	4%	1%	2%	3%	2%	2%	2%	3%
Capex (% of sales)	5%	6%	6%	5%	6%	6%	4%	4%	5%	3%	5%

(continued)

Appendix 6. Financial Indicators Related to the Income Statement

	2005	2006	2007	2008	2009	2010	2011	2012	2013	2014	Average
Dividend payout[a]	6%	11%	11%	15%	41%	20%	14%	16%	20%	20%	19%
EBIT interest coverage	8.6×	8.9×	7.9×	5.8×	1.3×	3.1×	5.2×	3.2×	2.3×	3.1×	4.4×
ROE[b]	28%	26%	26%	19%	5%	10%	15%	13%	11%	12%	16%
ROCE[b]	26%	23%	22%	13%	4%	9%	13%	9%	7%	9%	14%
Oil field services											
Sales growth	10%	29%	10%	17%	–6%	4%	39%	21%	6%	6%	11%
EBITDA margin	19%	24%	28%	28%	24%	22%	23%	22%	20%	21%	20%
EBIT margin	13%	19%	23%	22%	17%	14%	16%	16%	13%	14%	14%
Net margin	10%	16%	16%	16%	11%	9%	11%	10%	9%	10%	9%
Capex (% of sales)	8%	10%	12%	13%	10%	11%	12%	12%	9%	8%	10%
Dividend payout[a]	18%	10%	11%	11%	17%	24%	17%	16%	20%	23%	28%
EBIT interest coverage	14.7×	23.1×	26.6×	27.0×	16.2×	14.0×	17.5×	19.4×	16.6×	18.1×	15.4×
ROE[b]	22%	32%	30%	27%	15%	10%	14%	14%	12%	13%	16%
ROCE[b]	24%	33%	37%	32%	19%	14%	18%	19%	15%	16%	18%
Engineering and construction											
Sales growth	15%	38%	45%	0%	13%	–12%	12%	18%	10%	0%	17%
EBITDA margin	14%	17%	17%	18%	18%	19%	18%	18%	15%	17%	15%
EBIT margin	10%	13%	14%	13%	13%	12%	12%	12%	9%	12%	10%
Net margin	5%	8%	10%	9%	9%	8%	8%	9%	6%	7%	6%
Capex (% of sales)	7%	8%	10%	13%	9%	11%	10%	10%	9%	9%	9%
Dividend payout[a]	31%	27%	20%	20%	26%	34%	31%	28%	38%	34%	38%
EBIT interest coverage	8.0×	14.8×	9.2×	11.9×	11.7×	11.4×	11.6×	14.0×	7.9×	9.3×	8.8×
ROE[b]	14%	23%	28%	22%	21%	14%	14%	15%	11%	11%	14%
ROCE[b]	20%	34%	34%	27%	28%	20%	19%	18%	13%	15%	19%
Contract drilling											
Sales growth	26%	45%	25%	31%	3%	–7%	10%	18%	3%	6%	17%
EBITDA margin	35%	41%	46%	49%	50%	45%	39%	36%	39%	40%	38%
EBIT margin	23%	33%	37%	39%	38%	30%	24%	21%	25%	24%	25%
Net margin	17%	26%	31%	31%	27%	22%	16%	9%	20%	21%	17%
Capex (% of sales)	23%	37%	36%	34%	33%	28%	38%	30%	36%	40%	31%
Dividend payout[a]	7%	12%	16%	17%	22%	26%	44%	71%	34%	45%	26%

(continued)

	2005	2006	2007	2008	2009	2010	2011	2012	2013	2014	Average
EBIT interest coverage	8.3×	18.4×	19.6×	15.8×	9.5×	6.7×	5.3×	4.8×	5.4×	5.5×	7.7×
ROE[b]	11%	21%	28%	28%	19%	13%	9%	6%	13%	14%	13%
ROCE[b]	13%	23%	26%	25%	19%	12%	10%	9%	11%	11%	13%

[a]Dividend payout ratio is calculated as cash dividends paid relative to net profit reported during the respective calendar year.
[b]ROE and ROCE are calculated on average shareholders' equity and average capital employed, respectively, during each year.
Note: Please see Appendix 4 for a list of the companies included in each energy subsector.
Source: FactSet.

APPENDIX 7. HISTORICAL ENERGY SUBSECTOR VALUATION, ONE-YEAR FORWARD VALUATION MULTIPLES

	2005	2006	2007	2008	2009	2010	2011	2012	2013	2014	Low	Median	High
EV/Sales													
Exploration and production	4.1×	4.0×	4.7×	2.4×	5.1×	5.0×	3.7×	3.4×	3.8×	3.8×	2.4×	3.7×	5.1×
Integrated oils	1.1×	1.1×	1.1×	0.6×	1.0×	0.9×	0.9×	0.7×	0.7×	0.8×	0.6×	1.0×	1.1×
Refining	0.6×	0.5×	0.5×	0.3×	0.5×	0.4×	0.3×	0.4×	0.3×	0.4×	0.3×	0.4×	0.6×
Oil field services	2.9×	2.6×	2.5×	1.0×	1.9×	2.2×	1.8×	1.2×	1.5×	1.2×	1.0×	1.9×	2.9×
Engineering and construction	1.5×	1.7×	1.7×	0.7×	1.4×	1.8×	1.9×	1.9×	1.5×	1.3×	0.7×	1.5×	1.9×
Contract drilling	3.9×	3.3×	3.9×	2.2×	2.9×	2.9×	2.4×	2.8×	2.8×	1.9×	1.9×	2.9×	4.5×
EV/EBITDA													
Exploration and production	6.1×	6.2×	7.3×	3.7×	9.7×	8.8×	6.7×	6.7×	7.1×	6.0×	3.7×	6.1×	9.7×
Integrated oils	4.9×	5.9×	6.6×	3.6×	5.8×	4.4×	4.0×	4.5×	5.2×	5.4×	3.6×	4.9×	6.6×
Refining	7.3×	6.5×	6.2×	4.9×	9.1×	7.9×	6.4×	7.0×	7.4×	8.9×	4.8×	6.5×	9.1×
Oil field services	13.1×	8.7×	9.3×	3.8×	10.1×	9.5×	7.3×	6.9×	8.6×	5.9×	3.8×	9.3×	17.1×
Engineering and construction	10.2×	10.6×	10.3×	3.5×	6.9×	8.8×	8.5×	9.6×	8.7×	6.9×	3.5×	8.5×	10.6×
Contract drilling	10.8×	7.1×	6.4×	3.9×	6.4×	7.4×	6.4×	7.0×	6.9×	4.9×	3.9×	7.1×	16.9×
EV/EBIT													
Exploration and production	9.3×	9.5×	12.9×	5.7×	20.7×	17.7×	12.7×	13.9×	14.5×	11.6×	5.7×	11.6×	20.7×
Integrated oils	6.3×	7.4×	8.0×	4.4×	9.1×	6.4×	5.8×	6.2×	8.2×	10.3×	4.4×	7.3×	10.3×
Refining	7.7×	7.4×	8.1×	7.1×	18.8×	14.6×	8.6×	10.1×	11.3×	13.8×	6.4×	8.1×	18.8×
Oil field services	17.1×	10.5×	11.5×	4.7×	16.0×	14.9×	12.3×	9.8×	14.7×	8.6×	4.7×	14.7×	33.9×
Engineering and construction	15.6×	14.5×	14.6×	4.4×	10.6×	13.7×	12.6×	13.1×	15.3×	9.6×	4.4×	14.4×	17.1×
Contract drilling	15.8×	8.5×	9.3×	5.2×	8.1×	12.5×	10.0×	9.9×	12.8×	9.9×	5.2×	12.5×	32.5×

(continued)

	2005	2006	2007	2008	2009	2010	2011	2012	2013	2014	Low	Median	High
P/E													
Exploration and production	13.8×	10.6×	17.7×	8.7×	20.8×	18.4×	13.2×	16.0×	20.3×	12.6×	8.7×	13.2×	20.8×
Integrated oils	9.8×	10.2×	11.3×	7.4×	14.5×	9.5×	7.9×	8.3×	11.3×	19.0×	7.4×	9.5×	19.0×
Refining	9.1×	8.2×	9.9×	15.1×	13.4×	12.8×	9.8×	10.0×	12.1×	14.2×	6.2×	9.8×	15.1×
Oil field services	24.8×	14.1×	17.1×	6.3×	24.4×	22.6×	16.2×	15.3×	20.8×	12.5×	6.3×	20.8×	59.8×
Engineering and construction	19.5×	19.0×	20.8×	7.0×	14.7×	17.7×	15.5×	16.9×	16.1×	12.2×	7.0×	16.9×	20.8×
Contract drilling	22.7×	12.6×	9.7×	6.1×	9.1×	15.3×	11.3×	13.0×	12.8×	11.8×	6.1×	13.0×	55.7×
P/B													
Exploration and production	3.0×	2.7×	3.0×	1.6×	2.3×	2.7×	2.0×	1.9×	1.9×	1.6×	1.6×	2.0×	3.0×
Integrated oils	2.3×	2.3×	2.5×	1.4×	1.7×	1.4×	1.2×	1.1×	1.1×	1.0×	1.0×	2.0×	2.5×
Refining	2.2×	2.4×	2.2×	1.0×	1.4×	1.3×	0.9×	1.2×	1.4×	1.3×	0.8×	1.3×	2.4×
Oil field services	4.3×	3.4×	3.4×	1.4×	1.7×	2.2×	2.0×	1.4×	1.5×	1.3×	1.3×	2.4×	4.3×
Engineering and construction	3.8×	4.4×	4.6×	1.5×	2.6×	3.0×	2.3×	2.3×	2.1×	1.4×	1.4×	2.3×	4.6×
Contract drilling	3.6×	2.5×	2.5×	1.1×	1.5×	1.4×	1.4×	1.2×	1.3×	0.8×	0.8×	1.7×	3.6×
Dividend yield													
Exploration and production	0.5%	0.7%	0.6%	0.9%	0.6%	0.6%	0.8%	0.9%	0.8%	1.3%	0.3%	0.7%	1.3%
Integrated oils	2.6%	2.7%	2.4%	5.2%	3.5%	3.4%	4.4%	4.5%	4.8%	5.5%	2.4%	3.4%	5.5%
Refining	2.4%	3.5%	3.1%	3.0%	2.5%	2.1%	1.6%	2.0%	1.7%	1.5%	1.5%	2.3%	3.5%
Oil field services	0.0%	0.5%	0.5%	1.3%	0.7%	0.6%	0.7%	1.0%	1.0%	1.6%	0.0%	0.5%	1.6%
Engineering and construction	1.8%	1.2%	1.6%	4.3%	2.0%	1.5%	1.3%	1.5%	1.3%	0.0%	0.0%	1.4%	4.3%
Contract drilling	0.2%	0.5%	0.4%	2.3%	0.5%	0.9%	1.8%	1.6%	2.1%	3.9%	0.0%	0.5%	3.9%

Notes: Please see Appendix 4 for a list of the companies included in each energy subsector. All historical valuation multiples are based on one-year forward financial estimates.
Source: FactSet.

Made in United States
North Haven, CT
27 May 2023

37030472R10073